Y0-BGT-169

Life of Fred®

Edgewood

Life of Fred®
Edgewood

Stanley F. Schmidt, Ph.D.

Polka Dot Publishing

© 2020 Stanley F. Schmidt
All rights reserved.

ISBN: 978-0-9791072-8-3

Library of Congress Catalog Number: 2011905775
Printed and bound in the United States of America

Polka Dot Publishing Reno, Nevada

To order copies of books in the Life of Fred series,

visit our website PolkaDotPublishing.com

Questions or comments? Email the author at lifeoffred@yahoo.com

Tenth printing

Life of Fred: Edgewood was illustrated by the author with additional clip art furnished under license from Nova Development Corporation, which holds the copyright to that art.

for Goodness' sake

or as J.S. Bach—who was
never noted for his plain
English—often expressed it:

Ad Majorem Dei Gloriam

(to the greater glory of God)

If you happen to spot an error that the author, the publisher, and the printer missed, please let us know with an email to: lifeoffred@yahoo.com

SPECIAL OFFER

As a reward, we'll email back to you a list of all the corrections that readers have reported.

A Note Before We Begin the Fifth Book in the Series

Life of Fred: Edgewood. You may be wondering, what's Edgewood?

Thinking of *Life of Fred: Apples*, you might wonder if Edgewood is some kind of tree. It isn't.

Thinking of *Life of Fred: Butterflies, Life of Fred: Cats,* and *Life of Fred: Dogs,* you might suppose that Edgewood is some kind of insect or animal. It isn't.

Edgewood is a place. Some readers (99%) might not have heard of Edgewood, Kentucky.

WHAT IS EDUCATION ALL ABOUT?

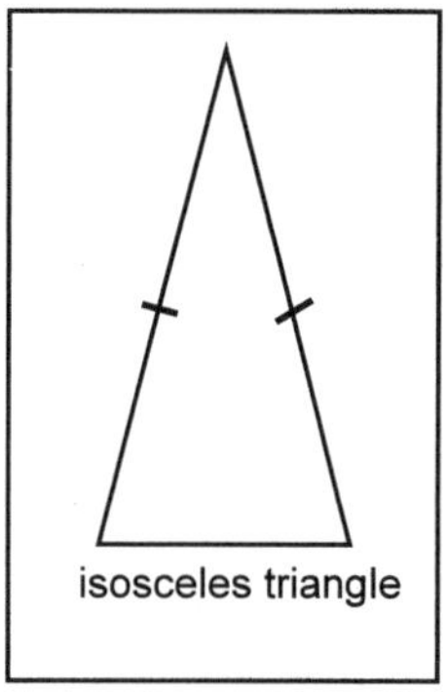

Years ago, when I was teaching a geometry class in high school, I drew an isosceles triangle on the board. (*Isosceles* is pronounced eye-SAUCE-a-lees.)

One student raised his hand and objected, "Mr. Schmidt, we haven't had isosceles triangles before."

I told him, "It's okay. It's something new."

He evidently didn't like the idea of learning new things. By the tenth grade, he figured that the rest of his life should just be a review of the things he already knew.

Education is new stuff.

Entertainment is ❖ hearing another rock band,
❖ watching another soap opera episode, or
❖ reading another murder mystery.

Of course, there's no law that says that learning can't be both. It is my hope that this book is both.

MATHEMATICS AND FUN?
YES!

It depends so much on how it is taught. I majored in math when I was a student at the university. I got C's in some of the math classes where the teaching was poor.

It's possible to make almost *any subject* distasteful.

Let's do **a little playing** and see how we could mess up the teaching of . . .

MUSIC For a list of 213 symphonies, you are required to memorize the composer's name, the date of composition, the number of movements, and the key signature. The test will be next Monday. (We choose Monday to ruin your weekend.)

ART For a list of 213 paintings, etc.

BASEBALL For the 213 games that the Edgewood ballplayers played from 1996 to 1999, you are required to memorize the final scores of each of those games, and the batting order. The test will be next Monday.

GERMAN Here is your vocabulary list of 213 words.

makaber = ghoulish
der Galgen = gibbet
denkwürdig = memorable
das Verhältnis = ratio
mit hängenden Schultern stehen = to slouch

The test will be on Monday.

PIZZA (This subject was hard to make boring. It took me several minutes to figure out how to make the teaching of pizza anything but delightful.)

Here is a list of some cheeses that begin with the letter G: Gabriel, Galette du Paludier, Galette Lyonnaise, Galloway Goat's Milk Gems, Gammelost, Gaperon a l'Ail, Garrotxa, Gastanberra, Geitost, Gippsland Blue, Gjetost, Gloucester, Golden Cross, Gorgonzola, Gornyaltajski, Gouda, Goutu, Gowrie, Grabetto, Graddost, Grafton Village Cheddar, Grana Padano, Grand Vatel, Grataron d' Areches, Gratte-Paille, Graviera, Greuilh, Greve, Gris de Lille, Gruyere, Gubbeen, and Guerbigny.

For each cheese, write a 250-word report that details how that cheese has been used in pizzas, its place(s) of manufacture, and current prices in major cities around the world.

On the other hand, learning is inherently fun. People love to find out new things. Some people will spend an hour each day watching or reading the news. Or watching quiz shows on television.

HOW TO LEARN FROM THIS BOOK

Please have a pencil and paper available. After all, this is a math book!

My daughter Jill

Write out the answers to each Your Turn to Play before turning the page and seeing my answers. Don't just read the questions and look at the answers. Not much learning happens when you take that shortcut.

CALCULATORS?

Not now. There will be plenty of time later (when you hit Pre-Algebra 1). Right now in arithmetic, our job is to learn the addition and multiplication facts by heart.

With my best wishes
for your adventures with Fred,
Stan

Contents

Chapter One
Wednesday Morning

Fred loved the early morning. It was one of his seven favorite parts of the day. Today was the 1855th day of his life.

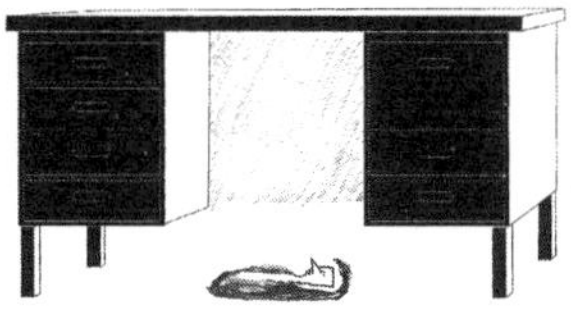

The sky was beginning to get light. Fred quietly got out of his sleeping bag and stood up. He thought of the day that he would be tall enough to bump his head on the underside of his desk. But today wasn't that day. Fred was much shorter than most five-year-olds.

He walked quietly to the window. He didn't want to wake his doll Kingie. The room smelled a bit because of the dogs that had been there. Opening the window, he let in some cool morning air.*

From the third-story window of the Math Building, Fred could look out over the KITTENS campus. In the early morning light, the trees were gray-green.

---

* For English majors: You don't write: *Opening the window, some cool air flowed in*, because that would mean that the cool air opened the window.

You don't write: *While brushing my teeth, the phone rang.* That says that the phone was brushing your teeth.

He put on a T-shirt, jogging shorts, socks, and running shoes and headed out the door. He walked quickly down the hallway past the nine vending machines (four on one side and five on the other), down two flights of stairs, and out into the semi-darkness of a February morning in Kansas.

Fred jogged through the campus. He passed the campus tennis courts and dreamed of the day he would be big enough to swing a tennis racquet.

He passed the university chapel where he attends Sunday school with the children of other faculty members.

When he got to the place where Tangent Road, Archimedes Lane, and Newton Street all met, he had to decide which direction to head.

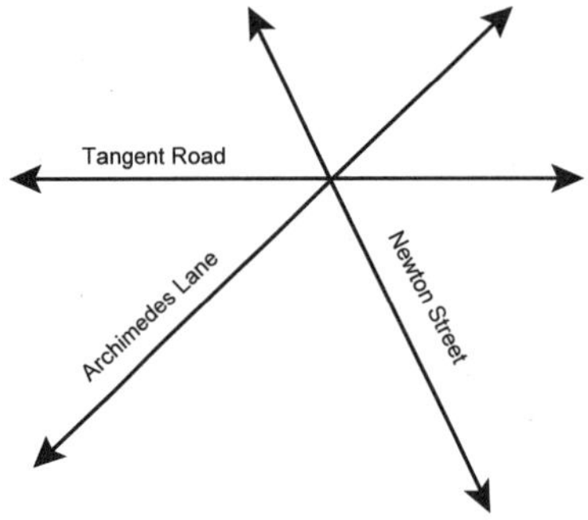

Lines are **concurrent** if they all meet at the same point.

Fred decided to head to the right (east) on Tangent Road. It was long and straight. He was warmed up by now and changed from jogging to running.

He felt the joy of being alive. As he ran the miles down Tangent Road, he let his thoughts just drift. It was a little like dreaming while you are awake.

❁❁❁❁❁ He thought of the Wizard of Oz play he had been in when he was in kindergarten.

❁❁❁❁❁ He thought of the kitty that he had owned on Monday.

❁❁❁❁❁ He thought of his geometry class and how he would present all the quadrilaterals (four-sided figures) in class today:

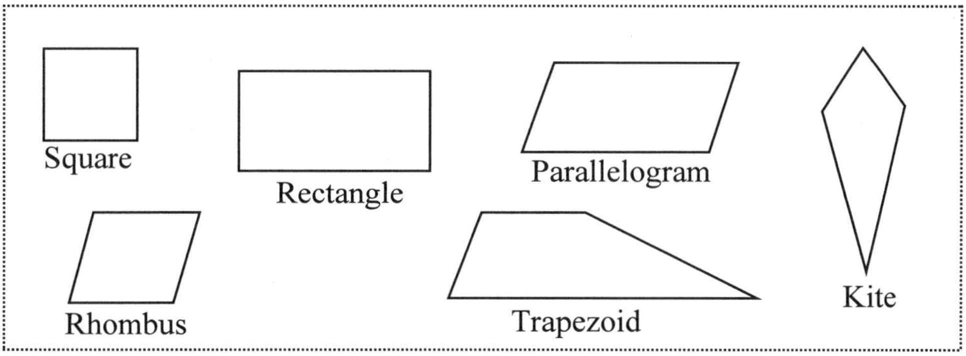

❁❁❁❁❁ When he saw the trees on Tangent Road, he thought of lines from a poem he had memorized:

> What can nestlings do
> In the nightly dew?
> Sleep beneath their mother's wing
> Till day breaks anew.
>
> If in field or tree
> There might only be
> Such a warm soft sleeping-place
> Found for me! *

---

* From Christina Rossetti's "A Chill."

❀❀❀❀❀ He thought that none of those quadrilaterals would make "a warm soft sleeping-place." They were too pointy. Instead, a nice ellipse made out of silk filled with cotton balls would be a nice place to snuggle.

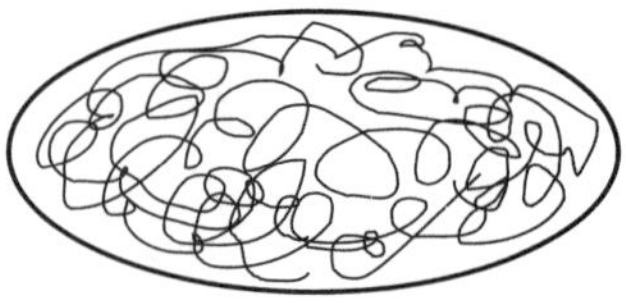

Fred liked to run east on Tangent Road. He could see the dawn of the new day. This was his new day but he was willing to share it with the seven billion other people on the planet. (7,000,000,000. Nine zeros.)

Fred liked the idea of sharing. He sang out a happy "Good Morning" to each animal or plant that he passed along the road:

Good morning Ant!
Good morning Butterfly!
Good morning Carrot!
Good morning Dove!
Good morning Eagle!
Good morning Frog!
Good morning Giant, long-tailed, big-toothed, two-horned monster.

Please take out a piece of paper and write down the answers. Then turn the page and compare your answers to mine.

You will learn a lot more by writing down your thoughts than just reading the questions and then looking at the answers.

Please.

Your Turn to Play

1. Just for fun . . .

Fred was creating a whole alphabet using animals or plants. He started with: ant, butterfly, carrot, dove, eagle, frog.

Instead of Giant, long-tailed, big-toothed, two-horned monster, he might have said hello to a geranium or a goldfish or a groundhog.

Finish his list, starting with a plant or animal starting with H and going all the way to Z.

You may need a little help when you get to U and X. The umbrellabird can be found in South America.

There is a frog found in the streams of southern Africa called a xenopus. Pronounced ZEN-neh-pess.

2. This is the 1855th day of Fred's life. Ordinal numbers are numbers such as first, second, and 1855th.

Fred is 1855 days old. What are numbers such as one, two, and 1855 called?

.......ANSWERS.......

1. Your answers will probably be different than mine. Here is my list of plants or animals from H to Z:

Hippo, hyacinth, hog
Ice plant, iris, ibex
Jasmine, jaguar, jerboa
Kangaroo, koala
Lotus, lion, leopard, laurel
Magnolia, mouse, moose
Nectarine, nasturtium, nuthatch
Orange, otter, ox
Panther, poppy, petunia
Quail, quince
Rose, rat, raccoon, rhino
Sunflower, snail, snake
Turtle, tulip, tangerine
Umbrellabird
Violets, viper
Walnut, walrus, weasel
Xenopus
Yak, yucca
Zebra, zinnia

jerboa

magnolia

viper

2. Numbers used in counting are called cardinal numbers.

The cardinal number associated with {A, ❃, ❂} is 3. The cardinality of { } is 0.

Chapter Two
Meeting Troubles

Do you know how difficult it is to jog when there is a giant, long-tailed, big-toothed, two-horned monster standing in front of you?

If you are alive, you will have giant, long-tailed, big-toothed, two-horned monsters in your life. They are called troubles.

How you deal with the monsters in your life shows how grown up you are.

This giant, long-tailed, big-toothed, two-horned monster that was standing in front of Fred was really big. If it stepped on Fred, he would be squished.

If it decided to eat him, Fred wouldn't be teaching at KITTENS University anymore.

Fred repeated his greeting, "Good morning giant, long-tailed, big-toothed, two-horned monster."

The monster didn't say anything. It didn't move.

Fred had a zillion thoughts:
Maybe the monster doesn't speak English.
Maybe it is asleep—even with its eyes open.
Maybe it can't hear me—or see me.
Maybe it is so grouchy that it doesn't want to respond to my happy "Good morning."
Maybe I had just better get out of here in a hurry.

Fred ran around the monster and continued down Tangent Road.

If he had looked back, he would have seen a different view of the "monster."

Moral: Most of the time
when we see some big bad
trouble standing in front of us,
it
will
turn
out
to
be
a
silly rubber balloon
when we look back on it.

Tangent Road was straight and long. Fred ran and ran.

This man was standing still in front of a do-not-pass sign. He wasn't moving at all.

Yesterday, Fred had seen that same man standing still in front of a stop sign.

It was a mystery.

Fred wondered if the man would get really old waiting for the sign to change.

Ten minutes passed. The sun had risen and was getting in Fred's eyes. He decided to turn around and head west on Tangent Road. Fred could have jogged all day. He had been running almost every day for most of his life. He was in good shape but he needed to get back to his office to prepare for teaching his math classes at KITTENS.

He passed the man who was still looking at the sign.

He got back to the intersection of Tangent Road, Archimedes Lane, and Newton Street and then headed through the campus.

In the sunshine, the trees on the campus had changed from gray-green to bright green.*

He picked up a copy of the campus newspaper. Fred was hoping that they didn't cancel classes again.

THE KITTEN Caboodle

The Official Campus Newspaper of KITTENS University — Wednesday 6:35 a.m. 10¢

See the World Program

Trips Assigned for Everyone

KANSAS: The President of KITTENS announced last night that he is closing the campus today.

Exclusive Interview with KITTENS President at Ski Lodge

From his ski lodge where he had been skiing on Tuesday, he declared, "Our students and faculty have not seen enough of the world. They need to get out and look around.

"Our campus computer has made trip assignments for every student and every teacher on campus.

"When everyone comes back, classes will resume."

The president will continue skiing while everyone is traveling.

---

* At least the evergreen trees—the ones that had leaves in the winter—were green. The deciduous trees—the ones that lose their leaves in winter—were not green.

Another mystery for Fred: He had taught for one hour on Tuesday and not at all on Monday. When would KITTENS allow the students to be in the classroom?

Your Turn to Play

1. Find the value of y that makes this true: $3 + y = 11$. (This means, "What would you add to 3 to get 11?")

2. What is the cardinality of {✐, ❖, 7, 💻}?

3. A rhombus is a four-sided figure in which all four sides have the same length. Is every square a rhombus?

4. A trapezoid is a four-sided figure in which exactly two of the four sides are parallel.

Parallel means they "go in the same direction." Here are two parallel lines:

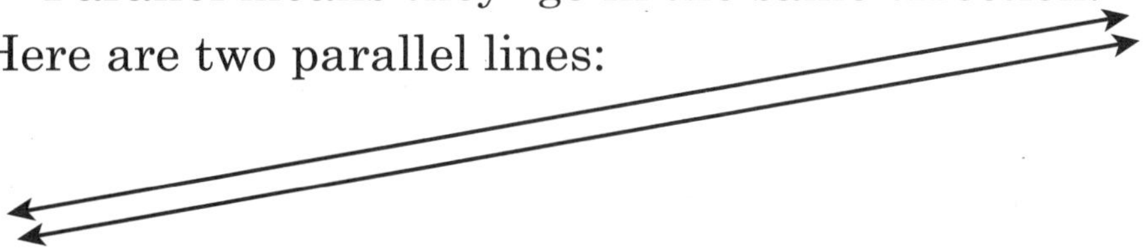

No matter how far you stretched those lines, they would never touch each other.

Most trapezoids have no right angles. Is it possible for a trapezoid to have two right angles?

5. Is it possible for a trapezoid to have four right angles?

........ANSWERS........

1. If y = 8, then 3 + y = 11 will be true.

2. The cardinality of {✐, ❖, 7, 💻} is 4. The cardinality of a set is the number of elements in a set.

The cardinal numbers are 0, 1, 2, 3, 4, 5. . . .

3. Is every square a rhombus? Yes.

All four sides of a square have the same length, so every square is a rhombus.

4. Here is a picture of a trapezoid. Exactly two sides are parallel.

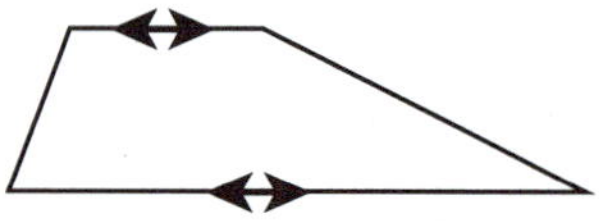

Can a trapezoid have two right angles? Yes. Here is a drawing of a four-sided figure with exactly two sides parallel and with exactly two right angles.

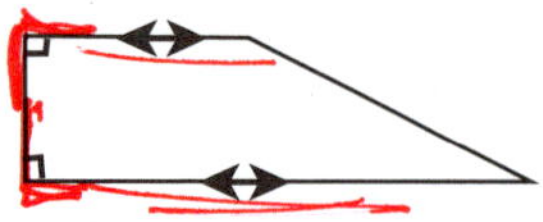

5. I can't figure out how to draw a trapezoid with four right angles. The minute I do that I have a rectangle. No rectangle is a trapezoid, because a trapezoid has *exactly* two parallel sides.

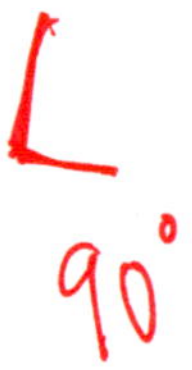

Chapter Three
Facing Your Fears

Fred entered the Math Building and ran up the two flights of stairs to the third floor. He was a little bit afraid to get back to his office. He knew that the trip assignments would have been sent out by KITTENS campus mail, and his assignment was probably sitting on his desk.

He stopped at the restroom to wash his face. He didn't normally do that after jogging. He was delaying the moment in which he would find out where he had to travel.

He stopped at the nine vending machines (four on one side and five on the other). He wasn't really hungry.

> Time Out!
>
> Have you ever been faced with something that you didn't want to do?
>
> ☞ For kids, it might be something like cleaning up their rooms.
>
> ☞ For teenagers, it might be a 15-page paper that needs to be written about the unconstitutionality of the National Recovery Act.

☞ For adults, it might be doing their income tax returns, or starting an exercise program, or writing a will.

People do one of two things:

① They postpone. Students will delay working on that 15-page paper all semester long. There is a dull, nagging ache that they live with for months, or . . .
② They face their fears. They start working on that paper, doing a little each day.

Your choice: ① postpone and live with the chronic dread, or ② conquer the dread and live happily each day.

By washing his face and staring at the vending machines Fred had delayed facing the pain by two minutes.

This was February. Fred wanted to be at KITTENS and teach. He didn't want to have to go somewhere else right now.

He opened his office door. There on his desk was a piece of mail from KITTENS University.

Kingie was just finishing up another oil painting and told Fred, "You'll never guess where you're going."

"Winter Cabin"
by Kingie

Kingie had read the postcard that had been mailed by the KITTENS campus computer and hinted to Fred, "It starts with an E."

Fred thought of all the places that began with E: *Maybe it will be to Ecuador. That would be nice. It's below the equator. It is winter weather here in Kansas, so it will be warm there.*

Maybe it will be to Egypt. Egypt is where one of the world's oldest continuous civilizations is.

Maybe . . . Fred stopped thinking and just looked at the postcard.

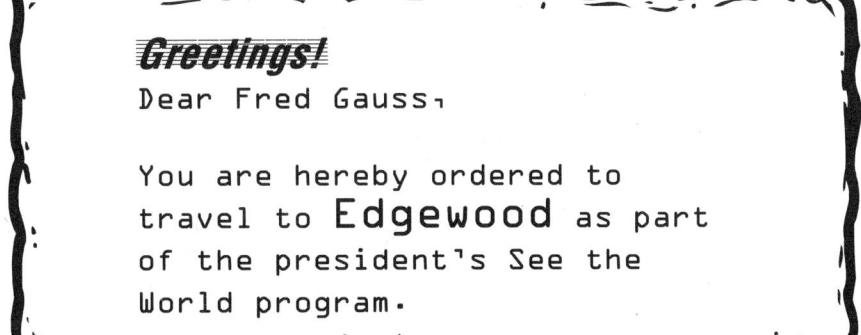

Greetings!

Dear Fred Gauss,

You are hereby ordered to travel to **Edgewood** as part of the president's See the World program.

"Edgewood!" Fred exclaimed. "I've never heard of such a country."

Kingie giggled and said, "Edgewood isn't a country."

"I wonder how the campus computer assigned me to Edgewood?" Fred asked. He wasn't expecting Kingie to know the answer. There was a function (a rule) which assigned to each student and each teacher exactly one place.

Fred's first guess was that the computer alphabetized all the names of the people and then took an alphabetized list of places. Then it assigned the first person to the first place, etc.

Alexander	→	Albania
Betty	→	Algeria
Carl	→	Andorra
Carrie	→	Angola
Claire	→	Argentina

Fred's second guess was that the computer picked significant, important places for each person.

Alexander	→	Berlin
Betty	→	Paris
Carl	→	New York
Carrie	→	London
Claire	→	London

> It's okay that Carrie and Claire are both assigned to London. It is still a function. If each person is assigned to exactly one place, it is a function.

That guess was probably not right. Who ever heard of Edgewood?

Fred's third guess was that tall people were assigned to places that everyone knows about and short people were assigned to less significant places. That would explain why three-foot-tall Fred was assigned to Edgewood.

Fred heard a knock on the door. It was Betty and Alexander.

Betty asked, "And where are you going Fred?" Fred showed her the postcard. He was ashamed to say Edgewood aloud.

Betty continued, "Alexander has been assigned to Asmara, which is the capital of Eritrea." This meant that Fred's third guess—that tall people would be assigned to more famous places—was not a good guess.

Your Turn to Play

Kingie made up some functions that were easier to guess.

1.

10	→	5	12	→	6	4	→	2
20	→	10	2	→	1	100	→	50
66	→	33	6	→	3	14	→	7

What is the rule for this function?

2. Kingie's second function concerned oil paintings he had made this morning.

"Winter Cabin" by Kingie → \$1600

"Kansas Skyline" by Kingie → \$1600

"Impressionist Dawn" by Kingie → \$1600

"Dog with Bone" by Kingie → \$1600

"Morning Cereal" by Kingie → \$1600

"Broken Skis" by Kingie → \$1600

What is the rule for this function?

3. A rhombus is a four-sided figure in which all four sides have the same length. Draw a rhombus.

. . . . ANSWERS . . . .

1. The rule for this function is *Find the number that is half as big as the starting number.*

Or you could say *Find a number, so that when you double it you will get the starting number.*

For example if you have 4 ⇢ ?, you would look for a number so that ? + ? would equal 4. The answer would be 4 ⇢ 2.

2. This is a constant function. The rule is *Every painting is assigned $1600.*

3.  or  or 

It's time for A Row of Practice.

Cover the gray answers with a blank sheet of paper. Write your answers on your paper. Then after you have done the whole row, check your answers.

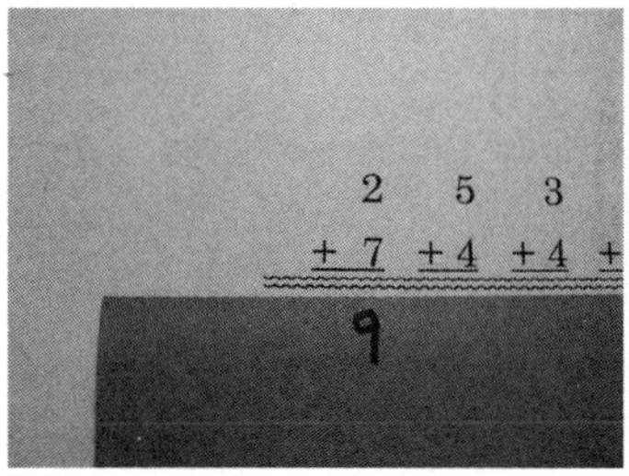

Something new: *If your answers are not all correct, then get out a new sheet of paper and do the row again.*

6	6	9	4	5	8	7	76
+ 7	− 2	+ 8	+ 5	+ 6	+ 5	+ 8	+ 1
13	4	17	9	11	13	15	77

Chapter Four
Where's Edgewood?

Fred couldn't figure out how the campus computer assigned people to places. He couldn't guess what the function rule was.

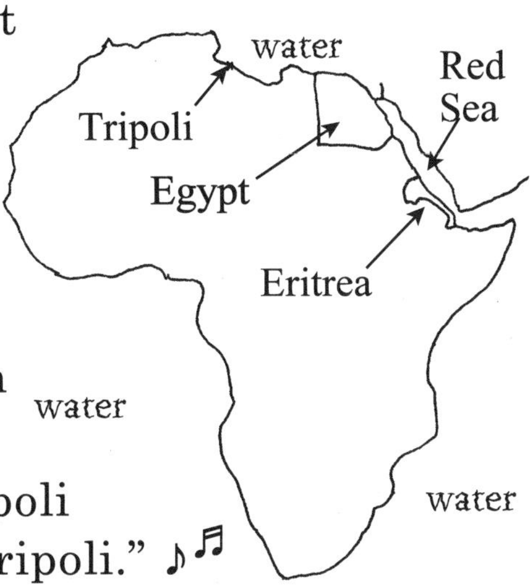

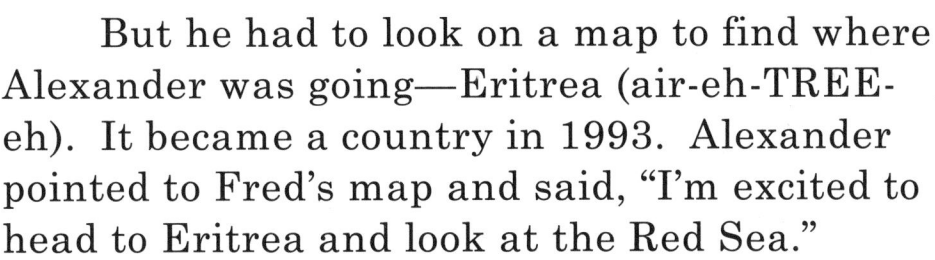

Fred knew that Egypt was in Africa. He knew where the Red Sea was. He had seen both of those on a map in Sunday school.

He knew where Tripoli was and "the shores of Tripoli." ♪♬

But he had to look on a map to find where Alexander was going—Eritrea (air-eh-TREE-eh). It became a country in 1993. Alexander pointed to Fred's map and said, "I'm excited to head to Eritrea and look at the Red Sea."

Fred asked, "And where are you going, Betty?"

She smiled. "I get to go to Scotland. It's north of Ireland and England. I can hardly wait to go there. Scotland has such a rich history and beautiful scenery."

Alexander turned to Fred and asked, "Where's Edgewood?"

Fred shrugged his shoulders. "I looked on the map of Africa, and it's not there. I looked in Europe, in Asia, in the Middle East, in South America, in Central America, and in Canada. I think it is going to be somewhere in the United States."

Fred was hoping that Edgewood would be somewhere in Kansas. Maybe it was close enough to KITTENS University so that he could walk there. Then he could make the trip quickly and get back home and resume teaching. Fred had forgotten what he had read in the newspaper. The president had said, "When *everyone* comes back, classes will resume."

The president wanted a long ski vacation.

Betty said, "We have to get going. We have to leave in about an hour, and we have a lot of packing to do."

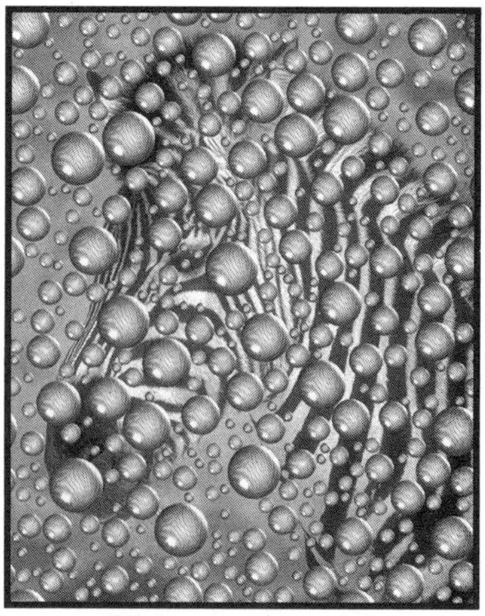

"Zebra in Thought"
by Kingie

Betty and Alexander left. Kingie was busy finishing up another oil painting. Many of the students had already left the campus.

Fred felt very alone.

He began to pack. He didn't know whether it would be cold or warm. He didn't know what he would be facing. He just packed the essentials in his backpack:

- a handkerchief
- a bow tie in case he had to teach
- a dozen books to read

He borrowed some money from Kingie to pay for the trip.* While Fred packed, an order came in on Kingie's computer. Kingie sold "Zebra in Thought" for $1,900.

Fred looked on a map of Kansas. There were a lot of cities and towns, but no Edgewood. His map of the United States only showed the bigger cities. He couldn't find Edgewood on that map.

There are no airports or train stations near KITTENS University, so Fred headed to the local bus station. He was hoping that they would know where Edgewood was.

He walked inside and said to the man behind the counter, "Hi. I would like a ticket to Edgewood."

* In the previous book, *Life of Fred: Dogs*, all Fred's money had been stolen.

"Edgewood?" He had never heard of Edgewood. He pulled an atlas out from under the counter and looked up the name. He looked at the alphabetized list of cities in the back of the atlas.

EBOLA, ZAIRE
EBOLI, ITALY
ECIJA, SPAIN
EDGEWOOD, MARYLAND
EDGEWOOD, NEW MEXICO
EDGEWOOD, TEXAS

"There's three Edgewoods. Which one do you want? Maryland, New Mexico, or Texas?" the man behind the counter asked.

Fred was silent. He didn't know what to say. Maryland, New Mexico, and Texas seemed so far away. He asked, "Is there anything closer?"

The man looked at the map for several minutes and found an Edgewood, Kentucky. It was so small that it wasn't even listed in the atlas index. He looked it up in his bus reference manual and told Fred, "There's this small town called Edgewood. Only about four square miles up near the northern end of Kentucky. It became a city in 1948. Only about 9,500 people live there."

Fred thought, *I like small*, and said, "One ticket to Edgewood, Kentucky, please."

When you are only three feet tall, *small* is sometimes perfect.

Your Turn to Play

1. While Fred was waiting for the Edgewood, Kentucky bus to arrive at the station, he headed to the public computer at the station and typed in `Edgewood, Kentucky.`

He found out: "`Males [in Edgewood] have a median income of $52,739.`"

Median income was short for median average income. Fred taught about averages in his arithmetic class at KITTENS.

To find the median average of a bunch of numbers, you first line them up from smallest to largest. Then you pick the one in the middle.

> Example:
> To find the median average of 5, 9, 4, 6, 3, you first line them up: 3, 4, 5, 6, 9.
> Then you pick the one in the middle, which in this case is 5.

Find the median average of 100, 50, 278, 13, 700.

2. Can a square ever be a trapezoid?

3. Fill in the blank: Numbers used in counting the number of members of a set are called ____?____ numbers.

.......ANSWERS.......

1. To find the median average of 100, 50, 278, 13, 700 you first line them up from smallest to largest:

13, 50, 100, 278, 700

Then you pick the one in the middle.

13, 50, 100, 278, 700

The median average is 100.

2. Squares have two pairs of parallel sides.

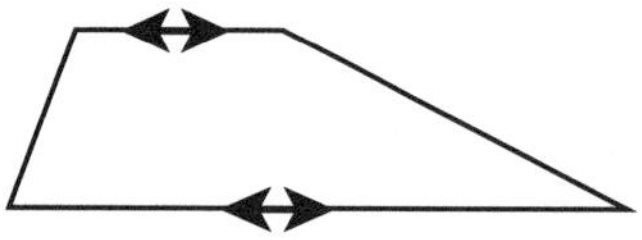

Trapezoids have exactly one pair of parallel sides.

Therefore, no square could ever be a trapezoid.

3. Numbers used in counting the number of members of a set are called cardinal numbers.

The cardinal numbers are 0, 1, 2, 3, 4, 5. . . .

This morning Kingie sold his "Zebra in Thought" for $1,900.

After Fred left for the bus station, Kingie painted and sold "Veranda" for $1,900.

$$\begin{array}{r} {}^{1}1900 \\ +\ 1900 \\ \hline 3800 \end{array}$$

9 and 9 are 18.
Write down the 8
and carry the 1.

"Veranda"
by Kingie

Chapter Five
On the Bus

With ticket in hand, Fred waited outside the bus station for the bus to Edgewood, Kentucky. He had forgotten to ask the man behind the counter when the bus was scheduled to arrive.

He pulled out one of the twelve books that he had brought with him for the trip. If you have a good book to read, the time can pass quickly.

After an hour, the bus to Edgewood arrived and Fred climbed aboard.

❀ ❀ ❀

This was a bit of good luck for Fred. The bus to Edgewood from KITTENS leaves on the second Wednesday of each month. This was the second Wednesday of the month. Had Fred gotten to the bus station a couple of hours later, he would have had to wait for a whole month until the second Wednesday in March for the bus.

Sometimes in life we get good luck that we really don't deserve. (That's why it's called *luck.*) And sometimes in life we get bad luck that we really don't deserve.

And, of course, many times we get *exactly* what we deserve:

- ✖ Stay up late at night and feel rotten the next day.
- ✖ Eat too much candy and get sick.
- ✖ Spend your money on junk and have nothing.
- ✖ Smoke and cough, cough, cough.
- ✖ Steal and get in big trouble.

Fred gave his ticket to the driver. Fred was beginning his trip in Kansas, which is in the middle of the United States.

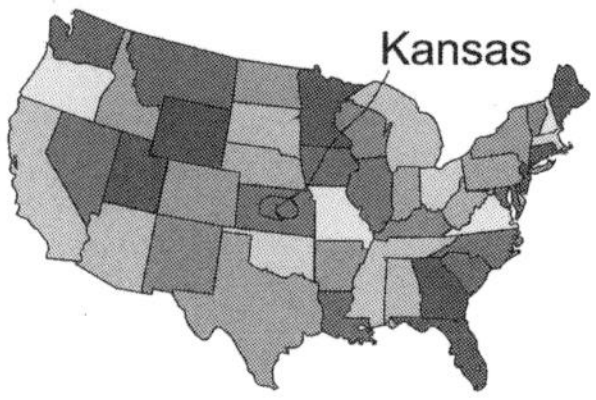

The bus would head east (to the right on the map) through Missouri and then into Kentucky.

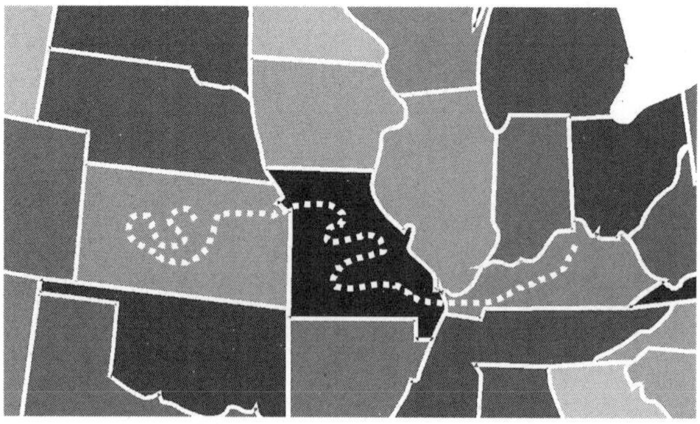

Near the northern tip of Kentucky is the city of Edgewood.

Fred headed to the back of the bus. Then Fred could see everything that was going on. He counted the other passengers.

As Fred thought of it: *The cardinality of the set of the other passengers is eight.*

Four were on the left side of the bus, and four on the right. 4 + 4 = 8. That was one of the doubles that he had taught yesterday in his 8 o'clock arithmetic class. He remembered how he had taught this in his class . . .

Fred finished washing the pans. He used four cupfuls of clean water to rinse out each pan.
Fred wrote on the board:
4
+ 4
8

Three of the passengers were wearing hats and five were not.

$$\begin{array}{r} 3 \\ +\ 5 \\ \hline 8 \end{array}$$

Two of the passengers were looking out the window. Six of them had turned around and were looking at Fred.

$$\begin{array}{r} 2 \\ +\ 6 \\ \hline 8 \end{array}$$

Fred became embarrassed. He didn't know why they were looking at him.

He knew that it was a little unusual to have a five-year-old get on a bus alone, especially a bus that was going to go from Kansas through Missouri to Kentucky.

Then he thought: *Is my face dirty? No, that couldn't be it. I washed it after I went jogging this morning.*

Then it dawned on him: He was still in his jogging clothes.

One woman said to her friend sitting next to her, "Do you see that half-naked four-year-old? He must be in some kind of trouble. I'll go back and talk with him."

Fred had heard every word. He knew that he was shorter than the average five-year-old. He knew that his arms and legs were bare. He knew that he didn't have an adult with him.

He had to think quickly.

He looked in his backpack. He put on his bow tie. *Now I won't look like I'm four-years-old,* he thought.

He thought of covering one of his knees with his handkerchief, but then the woman might think there was something wrong with his knee.

Your Turn to Play

1. Fred didn't realize that putting on a bow tie made him even more noticeable. All of the other passengers also turned around and looked at him.

How many of the eight passengers were *not* looking at him?

2. In the previous problem, you solved:

$$\begin{array}{r} 8 \\ -\ 8 \\ \hline \end{array}$$

Now let's do a slightly harder problem.

Find the answer to:

$$\begin{array}{r} 8609262942055 \\ -\ 8609262942055 \\ \hline \end{array}$$

3. 8609262942055 written with commas is 8,609,262,942,055 which is eight trillion, six hundred nine billion, two hundred sixty-two million, nine hundred forty-two thousand, fifty-five. (Notice that when it is read correctly you don't use the word *and*.)

Write out 5,024 in words.

.......ANSWERS.......

1. If all eight passengers were looking at Fred, then no passengers were *not* looking at him.

$$\begin{array}{r} 8 \\ -\ 8 \\ \hline 0 \end{array}$$

2. Any number subtracted from itself will equal zero.

$$\begin{array}{r} 8609262942055 \\ -\ 8609262942055 \\ \hline 0 \end{array}$$

3. 5,024 is written as five thousand, twenty-four.

It's time for A Row of Practice.

Cover the gray answers with a blank sheet of paper. Write your answers on your paper. Then after you have done the whole row, check your answers.

If your answers are not all correct, then get out a new sheet of paper and do the row again.

3	9	8	7	5	7	9	22
+ 5	− 4	+ 5	+ 8	+ 2	+ 8	+ 9	+ 2
8	5	13	15	7	15	18	24

Chapter Six
Fame

The woman walked to the back of the bus. She smiled and sat down next to him. There was a long pause.

Fred didn't know what to say.

She started the conversation, "Hi, sonny."

Fred wasn't sure what was happening. The other passengers were no longer looking at him. One of them had started to take a nap. Fred was worried that the woman beside him was some kind of bus policeman who was going to throw him off the bus because of his clothes.

Fred quietly said, "Hi."

"That's a cute T-shirt you're wearing. Do you know what it says on your shirt?"

Fred's thoughts raced: *She thinks I'm only four. She thinks I can't read. I've been reading for years.* He answered, "It says Math Prof.—KITTENS. Prof. is short for Professor, but professor was too long to fit on my shirt."

She said, "Oh. Does your daddy teach at KITTENS? Or your mommy?" She was trying to steer the conversation toward finding out where Fred's parents were.

Fred didn't want to go into a long discussion of his parents. He simply said, "No."

She kept asking questions. "Do you know someone who is a math professor at KITTENS?"

"Yes."

"What's his name?"

"Fred Gauss. His last name rhymes with *house.*"

"I've heard of Fred Gauss. He's the most famous math teacher in Kansas. I read an article about him last week. He has the most unique way of teaching mathematics. One time he pushed a stove into his classroom to teach the students that 2 + 2 = 4. There are two burners in front and two in back."

"I read that article also. It was in *Modern Math Teaching.*"

"You are only four and you read *Modern Math Teaching*!"

"I'm five. I'm small for my age."

"That Professor Fred Gauss is supposed to be five years old. That's hard to believe."

Fred couldn't stand it any longer. He said, "I am he."

She got up and ran back to her friend saying, "Mabel. It's Fred Gauss. He's right here on the bus with us. You gotta come talk with him."

Being famous is sometimes a big bother. People want to be near you just because you are famous.

Mabel hurried to the back of the bus to talk with this famous boy. She almost shouted, "Can I have your autograph?"

Fred got out his pen. He was used to this. He waited for her to get something to sign.

She ran back to her seat to find a piece of paper. All she could find was an old Saxon math book. Fred signed it.

After Mabel left, one of the other passengers walked back to Fred. He was carrying a clipboard. Fred got ready to sign his name again.

He said, "Hi. My daughter is studying advanced algebra. Here's a picture of her. She got stuck on solving this equation."

Here was something that Fred could enjoy. It was math.

The man showed Fred his clipboard. On it was the equation: $2^x = 5$.

The man was right: it was an advanced algebra problem. Fred explained that solving $2^x = 5$ would involve logarithms (LOG-uh-rhythms).

The man said he didn't know what logarithms were, but if Fred would just write out the solution, he would pass it along to his daughter.

**Warning! Do not read the next paragraph.
It is Advanced Algebra.**

Fred wrote: $2^x = 5$

Take the log of both sides $\log 2^x = \log 5$

Use the birdie rule* $x \log 2 = \log 5$

Divide both sides by log 2 $x = \dfrac{\log 5}{\log 2}$

If you want an approximate answer, you can use your calculator to find values of log 5 and log 2.**

The man thanked Fred and headed back to his seat.

In his classroom, Fred liked to use everything that happened to him in his everyday life as part of the teaching—even this trip to Edgewood. Suppose that during this trip 2 people ask for his autograph, 3 ask for math

---

* The birdie rule is the name that Fred gave to one of the laws of logarithms.
The rule is: $\log a^b = b \log a$.
You pretend that "b" is a little birdie and it flies down in front of the log.

** To find the approximate value of log 5, you simply press 5 and then hit the log key. The log key is found on scientific calculators. They also have keys marked sin, cos, and tan.

help, and 1 asks about his T-shirt. Back in the classroom he could show these things in a bar graph.

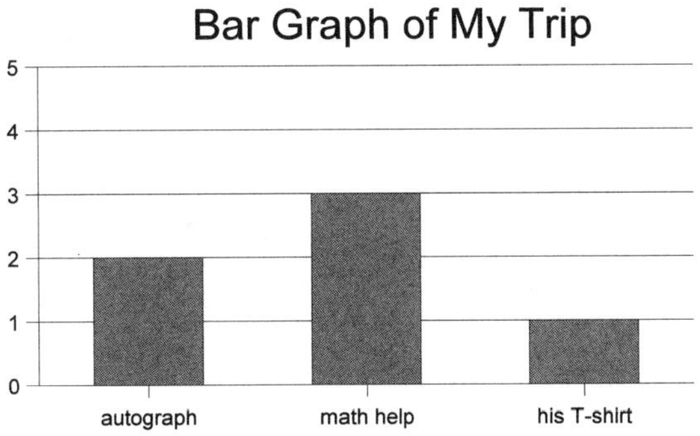

Many people would rather see a bar graph than read the words: *two people asked for an autograph; three people asked for help in mathematics; and one person asked about my T-shirt.*

Your Turn to Play

1. Draw a picture of four lines that are concurrent.

2. Change this sentence so that it makes sense: While writing on the blackboard, Fred's nose itched.

3. Cardinal numbers are used to count the number of members of a set. For example, the cardinal number associated with {C, D, E, F, G} is 5,

with {1, 2, 3, 4, . . . , 98, 99, 100} is 100,

with { } is 0,

with {❀} is 1.

How many cardinal numbers are less than 4? (Hint: the answer is not 3.)

4. Draw a bar graph to show: Joe ate 5 jelly beans, 4 doughnuts, 2 cans of Sluice, and 4 candy bars.

.......ANSWERS.......

1. 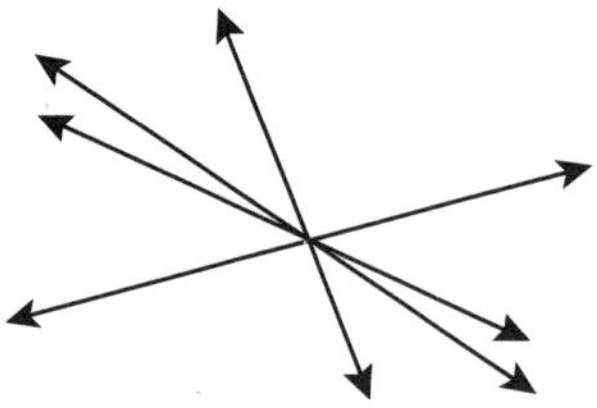

2. The original sentence (While writing on the blackboard, Fred's nose itched) means that Fred's nose was writing on the blackboard.

There are several different ways you can correct it. For example:

✓ When Fred was writing on the blackboard, his nose itched.

✓ While writing on the blackboard, Fred noticed that his nose itched.

3. Here are the cardinal numbers less than 4:

0, 1, 2, 3.

There are four cardinal numbers less than 4.

4.

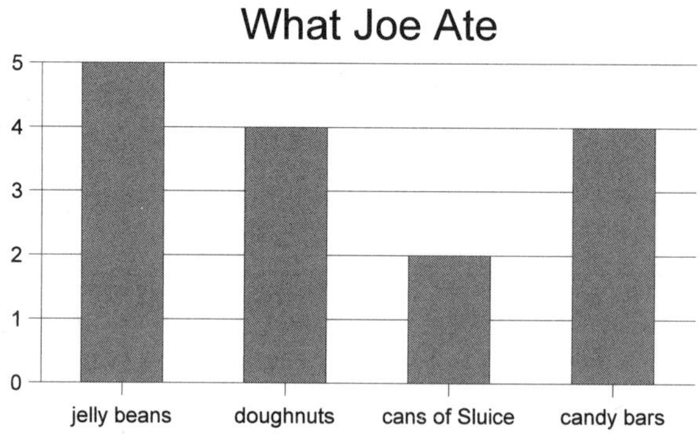

Chapter Seven
Reading on the Bus

Fred giggled. He was thinking of what a bar graph would look like if it showed the jelly beans, doughnuts, cans of Sluice, and candy bars that he had eaten on his trip to Edgewood.

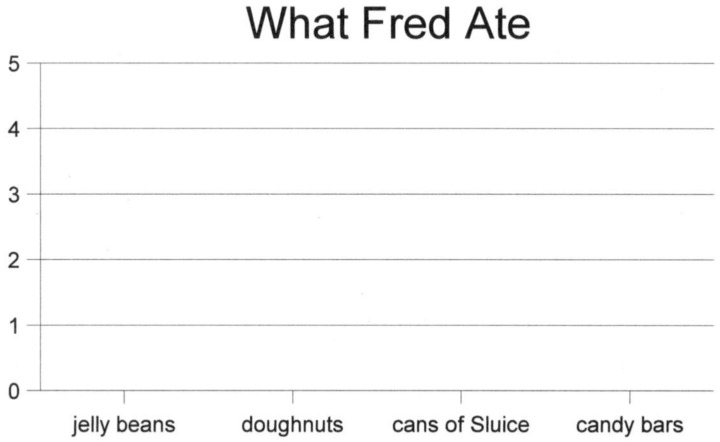

It would be a bar graph with no bars! Fred thought that that was funny.

Then Fred changed the categories:

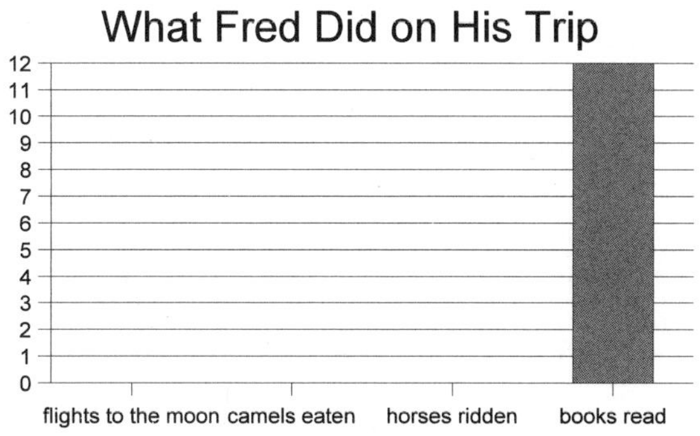

Fred pulled out another of the dozen books he had brought. It was *Introduction to Metamathematics* by Stephen Cole Kleene. It begins: Two successive eras of investigations of the foundations of mathematics in the nineteenth century, culminating in the theory of sets and the arithmetization of analysis. . . .*

Fred was excited. He had always wanted to learn about metamathematics, and here was his chance to read it uninterrupt. . . .

Someone tapped Fred on his knee. It was a little girl about two years old. She was almost as tall as Fred. She said, "Read me." (Translation: "Please read this book to me.")

She continued, "My mommy's asleep. So you read to me."

Fred put his metamathematics book into his backpack. He held out his hand, expecting her to hand him a book.

Instead, she hopped onto his lap and nearly crushed him. The thought of his being like Santa Claus passed through his mind—except

---

* That was the beginning of the first sentence of the book. (It's a real book. Metamathematics is studied at the graduate level in some universities that do heavy-duty math.)

The second sentence of the book is 62 words long: "The appearance in 1931 of Gödel's two incompleteness theorems, in 1933 of Tarski's work on the concept of truth in formalized languages, in 1934 of the Herbrand-Gödel notion of 'general recursive function,' and in 1936 of Church's thesis concerning it, inaugurate a still newer era in which mathematical tools are being applied both to evaluating the earlier programs and in unforeseen directions."

that he was too small to be Santa Claus and have kids sit on his lap. He couldn't see anything. Her hair covered his face. He asked her to sit down beside him on the bus seat "so that we can both see the book."

She took a book out of her pocket and handed it to him.

It was a very small book. It looked like she had carried it in her pocket for a long time.

Fred wondered how you could turn math into poetry for children. He opened the book and began reading.

6 + 5 = 11

Bread is made of flour
and leaven.
Six plus five is now
eleven.

7 + 6 = 13

My plate was full and
now is clean.
So seven and six will
add to thirteen.

9 + 8 = 17

John of Patmos
had Heaven seen,
And now I know
nine and eight are
seventeen.

Finding a rhyme for 17 was tough. —your author

8 + 7 ≠
15,000,000,000,000

Government accounting
can be thrillin',
But eight plus seven
ain't fifteen trillion.
(It's only 15.)

The girl pointed to each of the pictures when Fred read the poems. He wondered how much she understood.

He asked her, "How do you make bread out of flour and leaven?"

She told him, "Mommies do that. They take 11 flowers and stir it in a bowl." She didn't know that leaven is yeast or baking powder that makes the dough rise by adding little bubbles. Without leaven, bread would not be fluffy. It would be more like crackers.

Fred decided to play a game with her. He said, "Let's see who can name the biggest number."

She smiled and said, "You go first."

Fred looked at the last page in her four-page book of poetry and said, "Fifteen trillion."

She said, "Fifteen trillion, two. I win!"

$15{,}000{,}000{,}000{,}002 > 15{,}000{,}000{,}000{,}000$

$>$ means "greater than."

Your Turn to Play

1. A **couplet** is two lines of poetry that rhyme.

Bread is made of flour and leaven.
Six plus five is now eleven.

There are some words in English that you can't find a rhyme for. *Orange* and *silver* are two examples.

If you start a couplet with:

Once upon a time I ate an orange . . .

you won't be able to find a second line.

Finish these couplets:

I asked him please do tell me more,
When Fred said two plus two is ______.

Narrow is the way and the gate is strait,
And some can say that three plus five is ________ .

.......ANSWERS.......

1. I asked him please do tell me more,
When Fred said two plus two is __four__.

Narrow is the way and the gate is strait,
And some can say that three plus five is __eight__ .

This is a straight line: 

This is a crooked line: 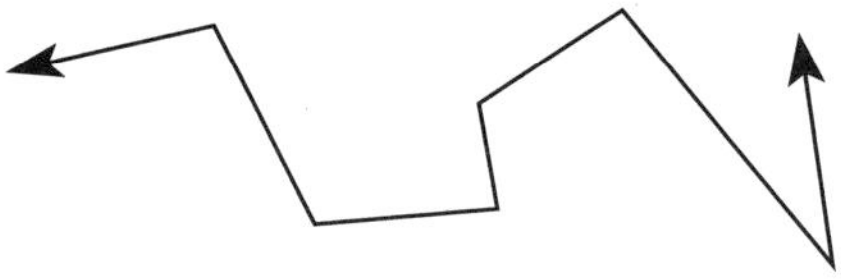

When they say that a gate is *strait*, they do not mean that it is *straight*.

Strait means narrow. Skinny. Strait gates are hard to get through.

To talk about a "straight gate" makes as much sense as talking about an "intelligent cheeseburger."

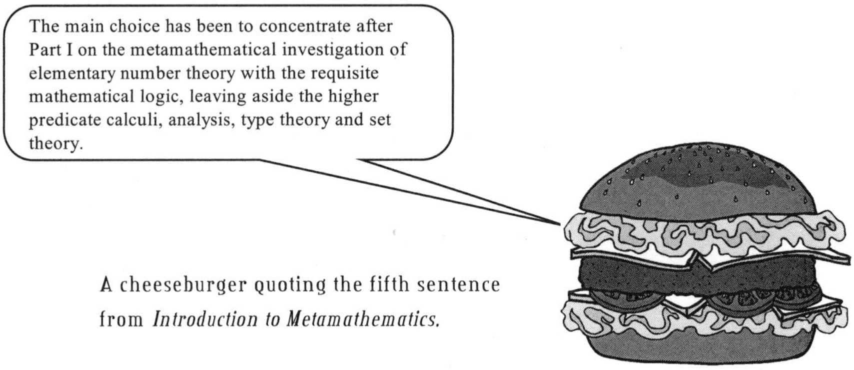
The main choice has been to concentrate after Part I on the metamathematical investigation of elementary number theory with the requisite mathematical logic, leaving aside the higher predicate calculi, analysis, type theory and set theory.

A cheeseburger quoting the fifth sentence from *Introduction to Metamathematics.*

Chapter Eight
Bus Stop

The little girl ran back to her mommy and woke her. She told her mother about beating this older boy in a math game.

Her mother rubbed her eyes. She told her daughter, "You shouldn't pick on kids who don't know as much math as you do. He's only about four years old. No one may have taught him about numbers yet."

Fred went back to reading his *Introduction to Metamathematics* book.

Moral: You shouldn't judge someone by his or her size.

The bus stopped just as they were leaving Kansas and entering Missouri.

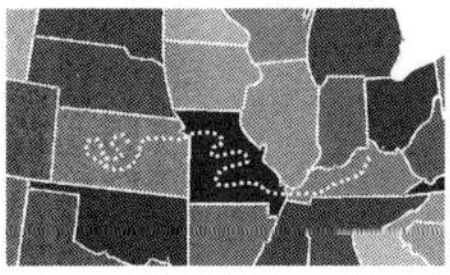

The bus driver announced, "Everybody out. This is our lunch stop. Please be back on the bus by one o'clock."

noon

It was now noon. Fred had one hour to spend.

Fred wasn't quite hungry yet. Rather than sit on the bus for an hour, he took his metamathematics book and left the bus. He thought *Maybe I can find a nice tree to sit under and read my book.*

The others rushed out to find a place to eat. Many of them planned to eat for 30 minutes and then shop for 30 minutes.

$$\begin{array}{rl} 30 & \text{minutes} \\ +\ 30 & \text{minutes} \\ \hline 60 & \text{minutes} \end{array}$$

Sixty minutes equals one hour.

Eating and shopping, Fred thought to himself. He pictured a tombstone:

Fred was only five years old and hadn't figured out everything about life. He knew that "He ate" wouldn't be on his tombstone. Instead there might be something about his love for his students.

It might say on the streets of an eastern town in Kansas . . . dressed in shorts and a T-shirt that read "Math Prof. KITTENS" . . . on a COLD day in February . . . three feet tall . . .

carrying a metamathematics book . . . wearing a bow tie . . . with a square head, a big pointy nose and no ears . . . thinking about tombstones as he travels to Edgewood, Kentucky—

—this is the only time in the history of the world in which this has happened.

Fred had 59 minutes left.

$$\begin{array}{r} 60 \\ -\ 1 \\ \hline 59 \end{array}$$

He had spent one minute thinking about eating, shopping, and the really important things in his life.

As he walked down the main street of the town, Fred was lost in reverie.*

If I were the university president . . .

Surprise! We are not canceling classes today.

* Pronounced REV-er-ree. Reverie is daydreaming, thinking pleasant thoughts, imagining fanciful things that aren't true today.

If KITTENS University were really big, I could have millions of students in my classes.

Fred didn't want fame for himself. He wasn't thinking of 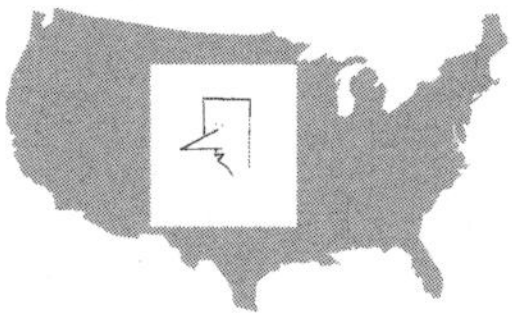

He wanted to have a lot of students learn about the wonders of mathematics.

If I were a writer, I could write a book about my doll Kingie and how he became an artist.

A thousand years, thought Fred, *would be too short to do all the things that I might want to do in life.*

While Fred is standing there outside the bus thinking about life, let's take a break.

Your Turn to Play

1. Find a value for y that makes 5 + y = 13 true. (This means, "What would you add to 5 to get 13?")

2. List all the pairs of numbers that add to 13. Your list might begin: 13 and 0, 12 and 1. . . .

3. On your paper, copy the ones that are true:

   5 > 2
   1,000 > 700
   0 > 4
   20 > 19
   8 > 3,438,995

4. What is the median average of 6, 2, 5, 5, 9?

5. Draw a picture of a square.

6. Draw a picture of a rhombus.

.......ANSWERS.......

1. 5 + y = 13 will be true when y is equal to 8.
When y is 8, 5 + y = 13 becomes 5 + 8 = 13.

2. 13 plus 0 equals 13.
12 plus 1 equals 13.
11 plus 2 equals 13.
10 plus 3 equals 13.
9 plus 4 equals 13.
8 plus 5 equals 13.
7 plus 6 equals 13.
6 plus 7 equals 13.
5 plus 8 equals 13.
4 plus 9 equals 13.
3 plus 10 equals 13.
2 plus 11 equals 13.
1 plus 12 equals 13.
0 plus 13 equals 13.

3. > means “greater than.” 5 > 2, 1,000 > 700, 20 > 19

4. To find the median average, the first step is to line up the numbers from smallest to largest: 2, 5, 5, 6, 9.
The second step is to pick the number in the middle.
The median average is 5.

5. 

6. 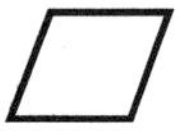 or  or 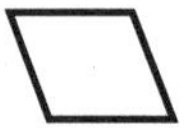

Chapter Nine
Into Missouri

Everyone was getting back on the bus. Fred had been standing on the street right outside the bus door.

Fred had *really* been lost in reverie. He had spent one minute thinking about people who spend their whole life eating and shopping.

He had spent 59 minutes daydreaming about being president of KITTENS University, about KITTENS expanding from the Pacific to the Atlantic, and about writing a biography* of Kingie.

$$\begin{array}{r} 1 \\ +\ 59 \\ \hline 60 \end{array}$$

It was now one o'clock.

An hour spent in pure thought is not a wasted hour.

---

* A biography is a story of someone's life. The *Life of Fred* series is a biography of Fred.

Fred headed to the back of the bus with his book. He hoped to get in some reading as the bus went through Missouri.

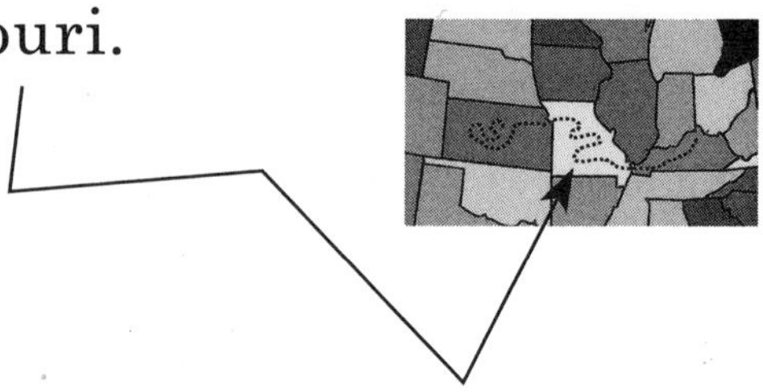

Fred opened his book and began to read the sixth sentence, "This choice was made because in number theory one finds the first and simplest exemplification of the newer methods . . ." when the two-year-old ran to the back of the bus to talk with Fred.

She pushed the book out of the way and said, "Hi!"

Fred put his metamathematics book in his backpack. He knew he wasn't going to get much reading done.

There are 550 pages in the book and Fred was in the middle of the sixth sentence. (550 is a cardinal number and *sixth* is an ordinal number.)

"My mommy and I ate lunch," she explained. "I ate a hamburger and french fries and catsup and a shake. Then I told mommy that I wanted a play toy for the bus.

"She told me I could pick out anything as long as it was under a dollar."

Fred thought to himself: *If* x *is the cost of the toy, then* $x < \$1$.

Fred also thought: *What can you get for under a dollar? It was probably some cheap plastic toy.*

Fred was wrong.

She continued, "We went to the pet store."

Fred thought: *What could you get at a pet store for less than a dollar? Maybe a worm.*

Fred looked out the bus window . . .

No, no, no, no, no, Fred thought. *Not a two-year-old with a mouse. Please! Not a mouse!*

If it's a mouse, I hope it's in a cage.

She couldn't have it in her pocket. Her pockets are too tight and small.

Maybe her mother has it and I don't have to look at it.

Fred was right about one thing: It wasn't in her pocket.

It was in her hair.

"Do you want to play with him?" she asked.

Before Fred could answer, she took the mouse and put it on Fred's lap. It ran up and sat on top of his head.

There are four emotions: mad, glad, sad, and afraid.

He was not mad.

He was not glad.

He was not sad.

But he was definitely afraid.

The two-year-old grabbed the mouse and ran back to her seat near the front of the bus. She was saying something about "Scaredy-cat, fraidy-cat."

Of the seven billion (7,000,000,000) people on earth, some are afraid of mice and some are not. Fred was in the first group. (Seven billion is a cardinal number, since it is used for counting the number of members of a set. *First* is an ordinal number.)

Fred's hands were shaking. He took out his metamathematics book and tried to read the sixth sentence again: "This choice was made because in number theory one finds the first and simplest exemplification of the newer methods. . . ."

What he read was: "The choice was afraid because the mumber hairy one fries the fish and. . . ."

Your brain can think, and it can feel. When your feelings (mad, glad, sad, afraid) are strong, it's hard to think straight.

Your Turn to Play

1. $<$ means "less than." On your paper, copy the ones that are true:

$3 < 11$ $229 < 97$ $0 < 4$

2. What is a rhombus called when it has four right angles?

3. List all pairs of numbers that add to 8. Your list may begin: 0 and 8, 1 and 7. . . .

4. What value of x will make $5 + x = 8$ true?

5. Finish this couplet:

"Mother, when will you love me . . . when?"

She smiled and said, "When five and five are ______."

6. [A harder problem] Is it possible for a trapezoid to have exactly one right angle?

.......ANSWERS.......

1. $3 < 11$ is true.

   $0 < 4$ is true.

> Two hundred twenty-nine is not less than ninety-seven. Instead, $229 > 97$ is true.

2. A rhombus has four sides—all of equal length.

If a rhombus also has four right angles, it becomes a square.

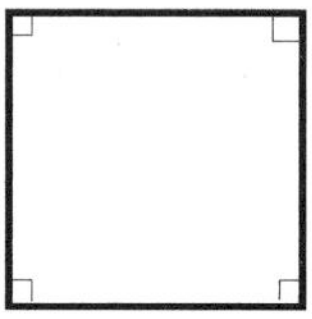

3. 0 and 8, 1 and 7, 2 and 6, 3 and 5, 4 and 4, 5 and 3, 6 and 2, 7 and 1, 8 and 0.

4. If x is equal to 3, then $5 + x = 8$ is true.

5. "Mother, when will you love me . . . when?"
   She smiled and said, "When five and five are ten."

6. A trapezoid is a four-sided figure in which exactly two of the four sides are parallel. I can't figure out how to draw a trapezoid with exactly one right angle. The minute that it has one right angle, it has to have a second right angle in order to make two of the sides parallel.

A Row of Practice. *If your answers are not all correct, then get out a new sheet of paper and do the row again.*

2	11	8	6	7	5	9	26
+ 6	− 6	+ 8	+ 9	+ 7	+ 8	+ 9	+ 2
8	5	16	15	14	13	18	28

Chapter Ten
A View from the Bus

Fred remembered the words of the university president, "Our students and faculty have not seen enough of the world. They need to get out and look around."

He hoped that the president was enjoying his skiing. So far, Fred couldn't say that he was enjoying his trip to Edgewood.

Fred counted the money that he had in his left pocket. $159.

In his right pocket, $66.

He added . . .

$$\begin{array}{r} {}^{1}1{}^{1}59 \\ +\ \ 66 \\ \hline 225 \end{array}$$

When you add bigger numbers, you start on the right side. Fred added the 9 and 6.

That's 15. He wrote down the 5 and carried the 1. Do you see the little 1 near the 5?

Then he added that little 1 to the 5 (that makes 6) and then added that 6 to the 6 and got 12.

He wrote down the 2 and carried the 1. He put the little 1 next to the big 1.

And finally, 1 + 1 = 2.

Fred had $225. He didn't know how long this trip was going to take. If it took a week, then $225 was probably enough money. If the trip took a year, then he would need more money.

He put the money back in his pockets and looked out the window of the bus. The president had said that he was supposed to see the world. He was looking.

He told himself a joke: *All I can see is scenery*. Since he was five years old, he laughed. He was starting to forget about the mouse.

This scenery looked a lot like the scenery that he had just seen in Kansas. Crossing a state line means that the laws may be different, but it usually doesn't affect the flowers and trees.

Top State Income Tax Rates

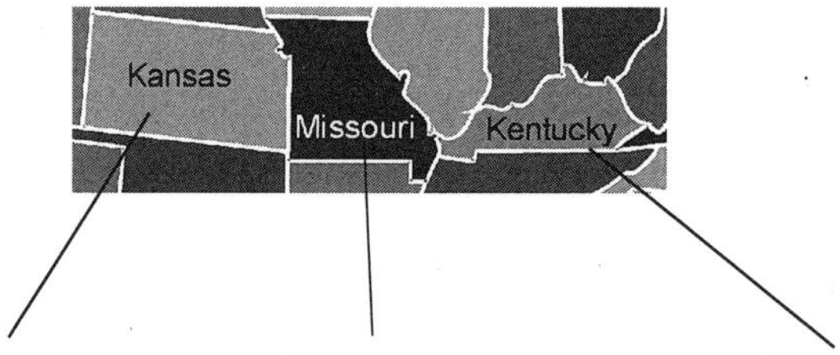

Kansas	Missouri	Kentucky
$4.60	$6.00	$6.00
per hundred dollars for income greater than $30,000	per hundred dollars for income greater than $9,000	per hundred dollars for income greater than $75,000

Some states have no state income tax: Alaska, Florida, Nevada, South Dakota, Texas, Washington, and Wyoming.

The cardinality of the set of states with no income tax is 7. {Alaska, Florida, Nevada, South Dakota, Texas, Washington, and Wyoming}

$6.00 per hundred dollars is sometimes written as 6%. (Six percent)

Personal Note

I, your author, grew up in California where the top state income tax rate is $13.30 per hundred dollars of income (13.30%).

Over twenty years ago, I moved to Nevada where the top rate is 0%.

Fred looked out the back window of the bus.

Fred did not see an empty road.

Fred did not see a Tyrannosaurus Rex running after the bus.

He did not see
a beautiful sunset.
Why?
It was only about twenty minutes after one in the afternoon.

If he didn't see an empty road, or
a Tyrannosaurus Rex, or
a lovely sunset,
there was only one thing Fred did see out the back window of the bus.

It was a glass filled with polka dots.

After several moments, Fred realized that this wasn't a 12-foot tall glass on the highway.

It was an 8-inch tall plastic glass that was sitting on the window ledge.

Your Turn to Play

1. If the tax is "$6 per hundred dollars of income," that means that if you make $100, the state government will take $6.

In pictures:

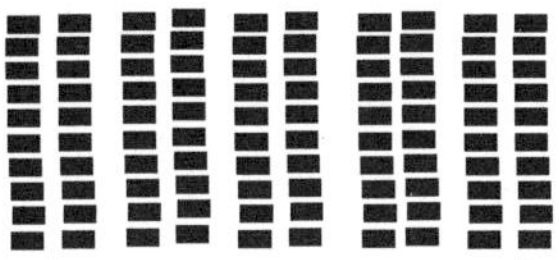

= $100 (ten stacks of ten)

State government takes <u>– $6</u> that's 6%

$94 you keep.

That was a state government tax rate. The United States Federal government's top tax rate (as of January 1, 2013) was 40%.

Your question: add 6% state tax
<u>+ 40%</u> federal tax

2. Can a square be a trapezoid?
3. Can a square be a rhombus?

.......ANSWERS.......

1. Adding

$$\begin{array}{r} 6\% \\ +\ 40\% \\ \hline 46\% \end{array}$$

One state government takes 6%:

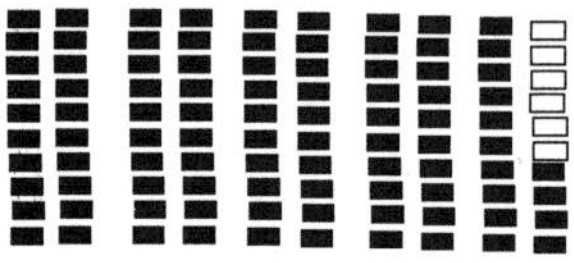

It's 6% in Missouri.
It's 0% in Nevada.
It's 11% in Hawaii.

The federal government takes 40%:

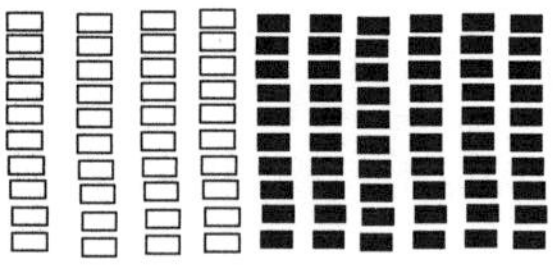

2. A trapezoid has exactly two sides parallel, so no square could be a trapezoid.

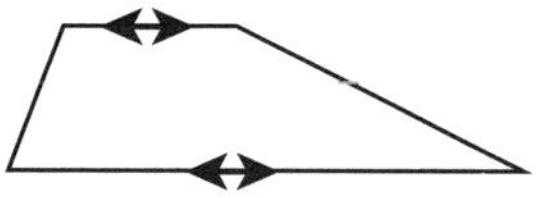

3. A rhombus has all four sides with the same length, so every square is a rhombus.

A Row of Practice

$$\begin{array}{r} 25 \\ +\ 54 \\ \hline 79 \end{array} \qquad \begin{array}{r} 47 \\ +\ 66 \\ \hline 113 \end{array} \qquad \begin{array}{r} 83 \\ +\ 98 \\ \hline 181 \end{array}$$

Chapter Eleven
A Glass of Polka Dots

Fred took the glass of polka dots and poured them out onto a piece of paper. *Yes,* he thought, *they are polka dots.*

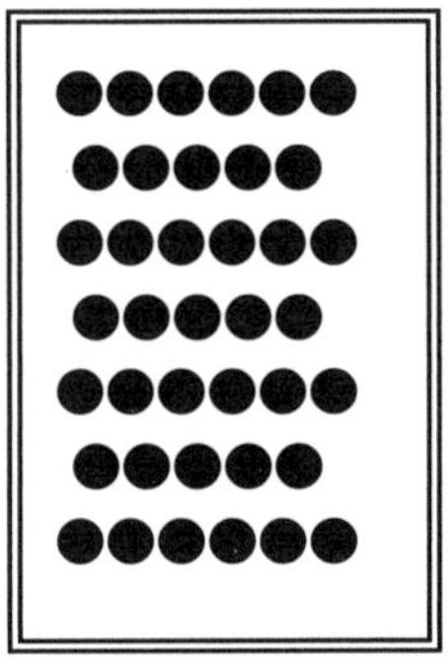

Polka dots on a sheet of paper

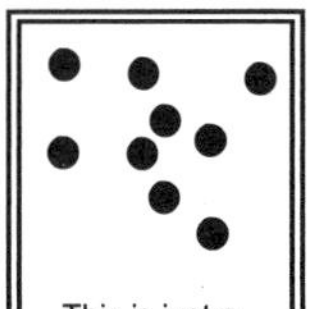

This is just a bunch of dots.

Polka dots are not just a bunch of dots. They form a pattern. They are in formation.

What mathematicians do is play. One way that they play is to find patterns.

Sometimes the things they discover feel almost like magic.

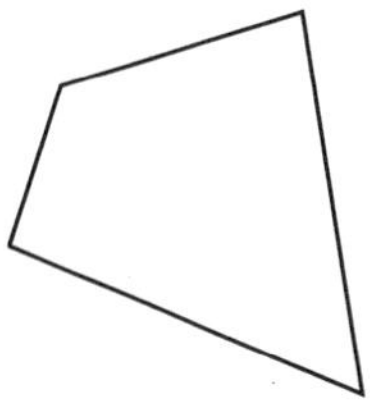

For example, take any old figure with four sides. There is a parallelogram hidden inside if you know where to look.

First, find the midpoints of each side.
(Midpoints are exactly in the middle of each side.)

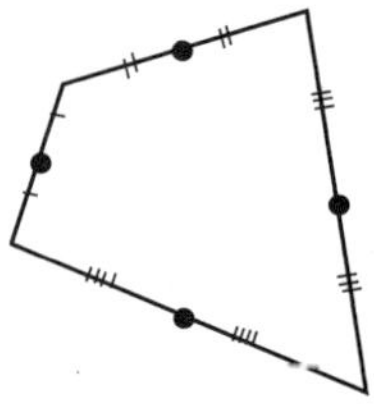

Then connect the dots. You get a parallelogram.
(A parallelogram has two pairs of parallel lines.)

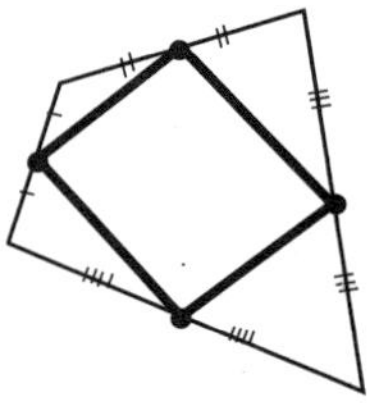

In *Life of Fred: Geometry,* we prove you *always* get a parallelogram.

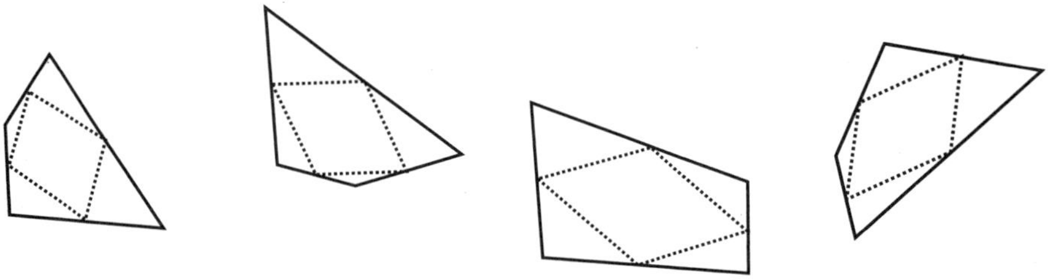

Fred took ten of the polka dots and put one on each finger. Some children like to do that with olives, but Fred didn't have any olives.

Then he stuck those ten into a single row on the side window of the bus.

●●●●●●●●●●

Then he arranged those ten dots into two rows of 5:

●●●●●
●●●●●

two rows

Then he moved the ten dots to make five rows:

He tried three rows,
but it didn't come out evenly.

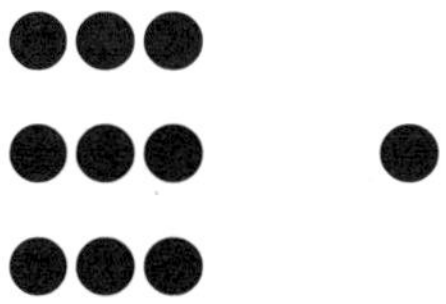

This is a **matrix**—a bunch of numbers arranged in a rectangle. This matrix shows the books that a four-year-old girl named Fredrika had in *Life of Fred: Advanced Algebra.*

This matrix has 3 **rows**. Rows are horizontal. ↔

In advanced algebra, you will also learn that it has 4 **columns**. Columns are vertical.

	algebra	geometry	trig	calculus
library books	30	9	5	70
books I own	1	1	1	1
borrowed from friends	10	3	2	8

Fred put the ten dots into two piles:

●●● and ●● = 10
●●● ●●

When the two-year-old saw Fred having fun with the polka dots, she ran to the back of the bus to play.

"Where's the mouse?" Fred asked nervously.

"Oh. I don't know. I think I lost him," she answered.

She pointed to the dots and said, "Share them . . ."

When two-year-olds talk, they sometimes leave words out of their sentences. When she said, "Share them . . ."

. . . she might have meant, "Would you please share the dots with me?"

—A Question—

. . . she might have meant, "Give those dots to me."

—A Command—

Questions and commands are two of the four kinds of sentences.

When she gets older, she will learn about all four sentence patterns:

❋ Statements (**declaratives**)

Robin had an 18" combination pizza.

❋ Questions (**interrogatives**)

Would you like some of it?

❋ Commands (**imperatives**)

Wash your hands first.

❋ Shouts (**exclamations**)

Ouch! (The water was too hot.)

Your Turn to Play

1. With the dots, Fred had shown that

$$\begin{array}{r} 6 \\ +\ 4 \\ \hline 10 \end{array}$$

Write all the pairs that add to 10.

2. Here are 100 boxes.
30% of them are black.
What percent of them are white?

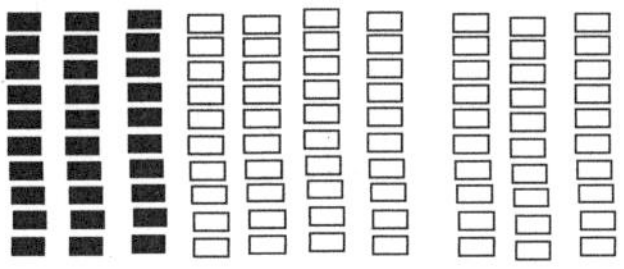

3. Is 2,986,885 one number or seven numbers?

.......ANSWERS.......

1. All the pairs that add to 10:

0	1	2	3	4	5	6	7	8	9	10
+ 10	+ 9	+ 8	+ 7	+ 6	+ 5	+ 4	+ 3	+ 2	+ 1	+ 0
10	10	10	10	10	10	10	10	10	10	10

2. There are different ways you could do this problem.

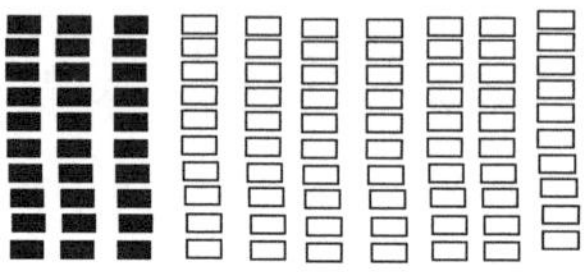

① You could just count the boxes that are white. Preferably, counting by tens: 10, 20, 30, 40, 50, 60, 70 and then say that 70% of the 100 boxes are white.

② Without doing all the counting, you could just subtract

$$\begin{array}{r} 100\% \\ -\ 30\% \\ \hline 70\% \end{array}$$

Starting on the right, you first subtract 0 from 0.
Then you subtract 3 from 10.

3. Two million, nine hundred eighty-six thousand, eight hundred eighty-five (2,986,885) is one number.

It is one *number* with seven *digits*.

Chapter Twelve
Sharing

Fred smiled and passed the sheet of paper with the polka dots on it to her. He told her he would be happy to share the dots with her.

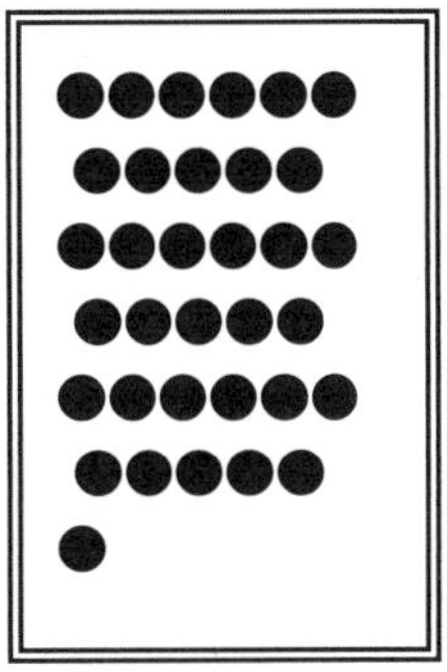

The polka dots except for the ten that Fred had stuck on the window

She took the ten dots that Fred had stuck on the window and put them back on the paper. She also grabbed the glass and took everything back to her seat.

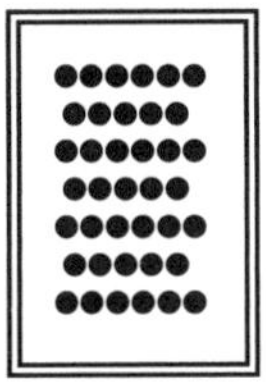

For some two-year-olds* *sharing* is what other people should do ⇨ **I get. You share.**

I and *you* are called pronouns. They help shorten up sentences.

Instead of writing:
Fyodor Mikhaylovich Dostoyevsky was a famous Russian writer. Fyodor Mikhaylovich Dostoyevsky wrote *Crime and Punishment.* Many people think Fyodor Mikhaylovich Dostoyevsky was a great novelist.

You could write: Fyodor Mikhaylovich Dostoyevsky was a famous Russian writer. He wrote *Crime and Punishment.* Many people think he was a great novelist.

* . . . and some grownups!

Pronouns come in three varieties:

First person: I, we

Second person: you

Third person: he, she, it, they.*

She had all the dots.
He had none.

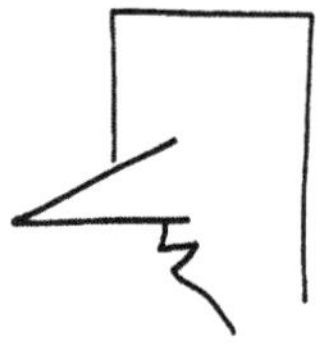

Actually, this is what Fred would look like if he didn't have any dots at all.

But Fred had many reasons to be happy. One silly reason that Fred thought of was: *I'm glad that my name is Fred Gauss and not Fyodor Mikhaylovich Dostoyevsky. I bet that it took him ten minutes to sign his name.*

Fred was just letting his mind wander. His thoughts . . .

Fred has 4 letters. Gauss has 5 letters. That's just like the vending machines in the

---

* English always seems more complicated than mathematics. Today, 2 + 2 = 4, and tomorrow, 2 + 2 = 4.

In English, they always seem to be changing things. Here is a more complete list of pronouns:

First person: I, me, my, we, us, our

Second person: you, your

Third person: he, him, his, she, her, hers, it, its, they, them, their, theirs.

And *its* does not have an apostrophe. (*It's* is short for *it is*.)

hallway of the Math Building: 4 on one side and 5 on the other. 4 + 5 = 9.

I had a student last semester whose name was Ty Lok. 2 + 3 = 5.

Fyodor 6

Mikhaylovich 12

Dostoyevsky 11

His name has . . .

$$\begin{array}{r} 6 \\ 12 \\ +\ 11 \\ \hline 29 \end{array}$$

twenty-nine letters in it.

If I were Russian, I wonder what my name would be? Fredor Gausskey?

Fred lay down on the bus seat and laid his backpack under his head as a pillow. He was soon asleep. And he dreamed.

And when you dream, your mind can really wander.

Fred's dream--

WELCOME TO DOTLAND!

Hello. I am your guide through DotLand.

I am a Duck named Dottie. Come with me.

This was a dream, so a duck with a bill and a

mouth didn't seem that strange. Having one leg in front of the other, however, was a bit weird.

"**We are going to fly**," Dottie announced.

Since this was a dream, Fred didn't think that flying was unusual. He wondered whether he would fly like Superman or grow wings and fly like a bird.  or 

"**Neither**!" Dottie told Fred. She could read his mind—something that can only happen in a dream. "**We won't fly the old-fashioned way. Climb in.**"

Fred thought, *I'm glad that Dottie, the duck from DotLand, is driving** *this plane. Or whatever it's called. I have no idea how all those dials and knobs and buttons and sticks and wheels and pedals work.*

Only one button was clearly marked. Fred wasn't very hungry so he didn't push that button.

Special Button

---

* The verb is *piloting*. You drive a car and pilot an airplane. If you had a ship, you could steer it.

Your Turn to Play

1. Fred asked Dottie what would happen if he pushed the "Cook the Pizza" button. She told him, "**First, the pizza would be thawed. That takes 6 minutes. Then it would be baked for 19 minutes. Then it would be cooled for 5 minutes and placed in your lap.**"

How long would these three things take?

$$\begin{array}{r} 6 \\ 19 \\ +\ 5 \\ \hline \end{array}$$

2. English can sometimes be a little silly. Which one of these is wrong?

- ❖ Flies fly.
- ❖ Drivers drive cars.
- ❖ Pilots pilot planes.
- ❖ Steers steer ships.
- ❖ Singers sing songs.

3. This is one-quarter of an hour. If you count by fives, (5, 10, 15), you can see that one-quarter of an hour is 15 minutes.

How many minutes are in half an hour?

.......ANSWERS.......

1. To add numbers with more than one digit, you start on the right column.

$$\begin{array}{r} 6 \\ \overset{2}{1}9 \\ +\ 5 \\ \hline 30 \end{array} \text{ minutes}$$

You add the 6 and 9. That makes 15.
15 and 5 make 20.
You write down the 0 and carry the 2.
2 and 1 make 3.

2. 

3. Half an hour is 30 minutes.

This is "half past three" or 3:30.

Chapter Thirteen
Flying

Dottie piloted the plane high above the freeway. Fred looked down. He could see the bus speeding along the road toward Kentucky.

The duck told him, "**Now I am going to show you some real flying!**"

They dove down near the bus.

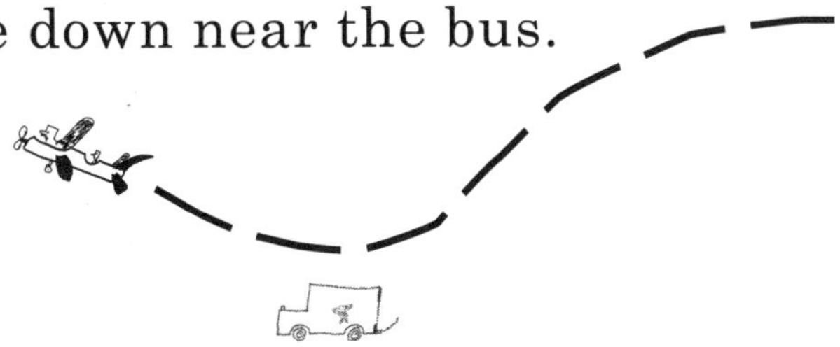

The two-year-old waved at them.

The duck made loops and then flew the plane upside down.

"**I hope you remembered to fasten your seat belt**," Dottie said.

Even in your dreams, it is good to buckle up.

Fred awoke with a thud. He had fallen off the bus seat.

The two-year-old ran to the back of the bus and put a dot on Fred's forehead.

She said, "All better now."

Before Fred could say thank you, she ran back to her seat.

The bus stopped.

Fred looked out the window. They were stopped on the side of the freeway. He couldn't see why they had stopped.

Everyone was quiet.

The bus driver stood up and said, "Hey folks. I can't figure it out. It looks like we've run outta gas.* I just filled her up in Kansas. I don't know what to make of this."

The bus driver opened the door and headed outside to see what was wrong. Fred and a couple of other passengers followed him.

The smell was strong. The fuel line had broken.

One man suggested, "You could just tape it. It would probably hold till we get to the next town. Then they could fix it."

---

* He meant diesel. Big buses usually don't run on gasoline.

The bus driver laughed. "Tape it? That would work—I've got some duct tape—but, hey, we don't have any gas left."

Everyone was quiet again.

Then the little kid with the big dot on his forehead asked, "How far is it to the nearest town? I'm a good jogger. I can get there pretty fast." Fred looked at the big tummy on the bus driver and knew that he, instead of the driver, should be the one to run to the town.

"About ten miles," the bus driver said.

Before another word could be spoken, Fred started running down the road.

Ten miles ahead, Fred thought to himself. *That's an easy jog. I jog at 5 miles per hour. It will only take me two hours to get there. Then I can get a repairman to come and fix the bus and put in some gas.*

Time Out!

Sometimes we make mistakes—even when we are trying to do good.

His smallest mistake was that he forgot to take the big dot off of his forehead.

His medium-sized mistake was that he forgot that some people carry cell phones.

The bus driver climbed back on the bus and asked, “Anybody got a cell phone? I forgot to charge mine.”

The two-year-old handed the driver her cell phone. It was pink and covered with big black dots.

The bus driver peeled off the dots and phoned for help.

Time Out!

Fred’s big mistake came because he got so excited that he didn’t pay attention.

He had asked, “How far is it to the nearest town?”

The bus driver had said, “About ten miles.”

Before another word could be spoken, Fred dashed down the road thinking *ten miles ahead.*

The bus driver was pointing back where they had come from.

Ahead, there was no town for another 40 miles.

Your Turn to Play

1. If Fred can jog at the rate of 5 miles per hour, how long would it take for him to jog 40 miles?

One way to do this is to count by fives.

5 10 15 . . .

ONE TWO THREE . . .

2. Draw a picture of a clock that reads half past two.

3. Here are 100 boxes. What percent of them are white?

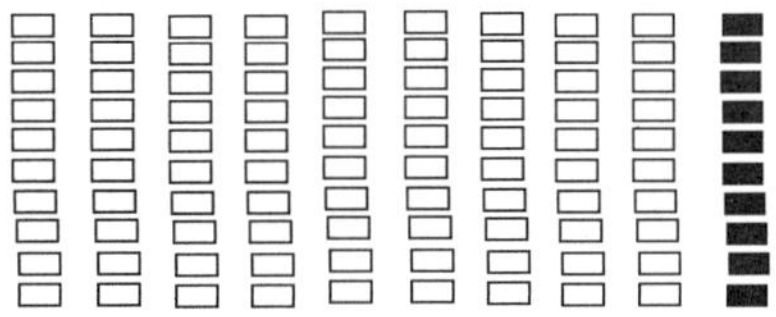

4. Name the largest number that has 3 digits in it.

5. Draw a bar graph to show: the distance to the nearest town (10 miles) and the distance to the town that Fred is jogging toward (40 miles).

ANSWERS

1. 5 10 15 20 25 30 35 40

ONE TWO THREE FOUR FIVE SIX SEVEN EIGHT

It takes eight 5s to make 40.

Jogging at the rate of 5 miles per hour, it will take Fred eight hours to go 40 miles.

2. Half past two is the same as 2:30.

2:30

3. One way to find out what percent of the 100 boxes are white would be to count the white boxes. (It would be fastest to count by tens.)

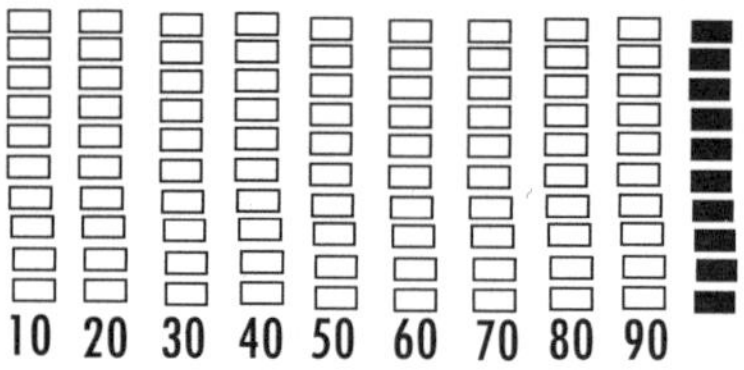

A second way would be to count the black boxes. There are 10 of them and then subtract:

$$\begin{array}{r} 100 \\ -\ 10 \\ \hline 90 \end{array}$$

Ninety percent of the boxes are white.

4. The largest number with three digits is 999.

5.

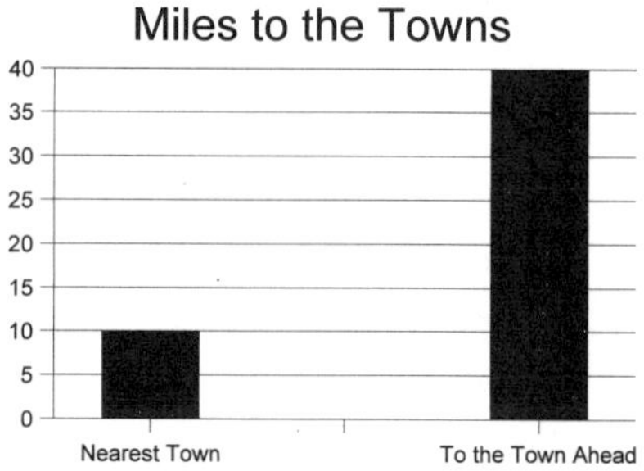

Chapter Fourteen
Food and Warmth

It was now a quarter after four. The bus driver called the auto repair place that was in the town ten miles in back of them.

He explained to the repairman that he had a busted* fuel line. He explained that he was ten miles east of the town.

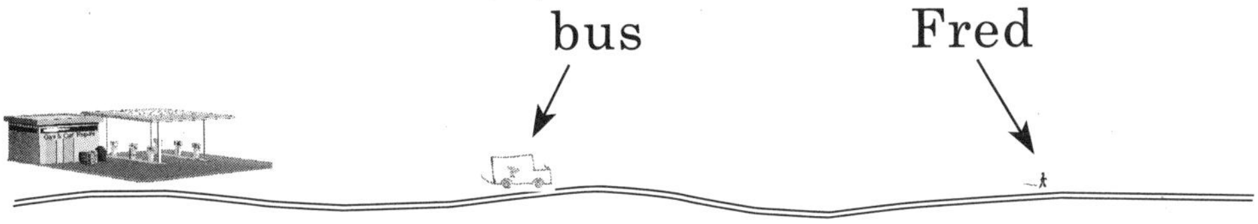

"Well . . . I can get one of the boys out there with a tow truck in under an hour. Fixin' a busted fuel line ain't no big deal."**

"Thanks. My eight passengers and I would really appreciate that."

---

* Using informal language, you might say *busted*. If you have some education, you would probably say *broken*.

** = "Repairing a broken fuel line is not difficult."

"Nine of you! What kind of car are you driving?"

"Didn't I say? It's not a car. It's a bus."

"Our tow truck is for cars. It can't pick up a bus. Tell you what. I'll have Max come out and do the repair right there. He can bring a big jack and all the tools."

"Great! When can we expect Max?"

"First thing in the morning. He's tied up with work here in the shop today."

"Okay. We'll see Max in the morning."

The driver handed the pink phone back to the two-year-old. He told his passengers that they would have to be doing some "camping" until morning.

He said that there were some emergency blankets stowed on the bus so they could keep warm during the night.

"But what about dinner?" the mother of the two-year-old asked.

The bus driver pointed to the dinner basket that his wife had packed for him:

An evening meal for the bus driver

A turkey, a quart of milk, three loaves of french bread, a salad in a plastic box, a bottle of apple juice, a jar of pickles, various sandwiches (tuna; bacon, lettuce and tomato; peanut butter and jelly; ham and cheese), a peach pie, and a half dozen cupcakes.

> A half dozen means one-half of a dozen.
>
> This means $\frac{1}{2}$ of 12.
>
> Or $\begin{array}{r} 6 \\ 2\overline{)\,12} \end{array}$
>
> Or 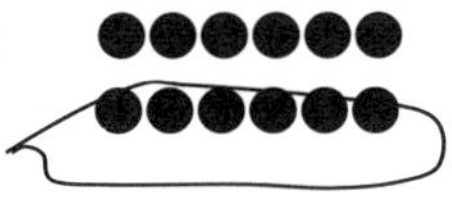

That was 9,000 calories to be divided up among nine people (the bus driver and the eight passengers).

Each would get a thousand calories of food.

$$\begin{array}{r} 1{,}000 \\ 1{,}000 \\ 1{,}000 \\ 1{,}000 \\ 1{,}000 \\ 1{,}000 \\ 1{,}000 \\ 1{,}000 \\ +\ 1{,}000 \\ \hline 9{,}000 \end{array}$$

Everyone would be well-fed and warm. Except . . .

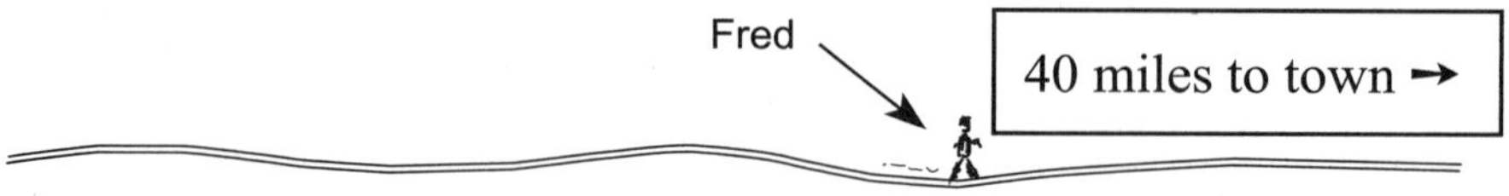

It was approaching dusk.* In Missouri in February, Fred figured that it must be around 6 p.m. Dressed only in a T-shirt and shorts, Fred was hoping that the town would be just over the next hill. It was starting to get cold. The black dot on his forehead wouldn't keep him very warm.

He ran for another half hour. (30 minutes)

1. *Maybe there will be a full moon,* Fred thought. *Then there would be enough light to keep on running.*

◄◄◄ Phases of the Moon ►►►

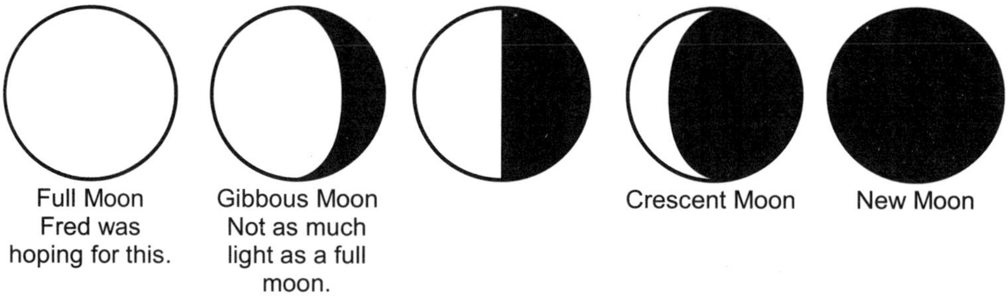

Tonight the moon gave no light.

---

* Dusk = darkness. From the Latin *fuscus*, which means dark or black.

Your Turn to Play

1. As Fred jogged in the semi-darkness, he thought of what he might be teaching back at KITTENS after he returned from Edgewood.

He had taught all the doubles: $1 + 1 = 2$

$2 + 2 = 4$

$6 + 6 = 12$

He could now teach about taking half of a number.

For example, half of 12 is 6 (since $6 + 6 = 12$).

What is half of 18?

2. Name the smallest number that has seven digits.
3. What is half of 100?
4. Draw a picture of a clock that reads half past eight.
5. How many nickels in 40¢? (Count by fives.)
6. Here is how you double 17.

$$\begin{array}{r} \overset{1}{1}7 \\ +\ 17 \\ \hline 34 \end{array}$$

You start on the right. $7 + 7 = 14$

Write down the 4 and carry the one.

$1 + 1 + 1 = 3$

What is 19 doubled?

. . . . ANSWERS . . . .

1. Half of 18 is 9 (since 9 + 9 = 18).

2. The smallest number with seven digits is one million (1,000,000).

3. Half of 100 is 50.

$$\begin{array}{r} 50 \\ +\ 50 \\ \hline 100 \end{array}$$

4. At 8:30, the big hand is on the 6 and the little hand is between 8 and 9.

5.

5	10	15	20	25	30	35	40
ONE	TWO	THREE	FOUR	FIVE	SIX	SEVEN	EIGHT

There are eight nickels in 40 cents.

6.

$$\begin{array}{r} {}^{1}19 \\ +\ 19 \\ \hline 38 \end{array}$$

You start on the right. 9 + 9 = 18
Write down the 8 and carry the one.
1 + 1 + 1 = 3

19 doubled is 38.

Chapter Fifteen
Errors

Fred stopped thinking about doubling numbers. He was thinking about how long ten miles is. He had often gone on ten-mile jogs in the morning when he was at KITTENS. He wondered, *Is ten miles longer in Missouri than in Kansas?*

He had to concentrate to stay on the roadway. Twice, in the darkness, he started to run off onto the shoulder of the road.

He thought about turning around and heading back to the bus, but he knew that he must be very close to the town. He knew that he had been running for about two hours. He knew that he ran at the rate of about 5 miles per hour. And the bus driver had told him that the town was about ten miles away.

Time Out!

There are two kinds of errors: Type One and Type Two.

A Type One error is when you don't know something.

A Type Two error is when you know something, and it is not true.

Fred knew that the town was ten miles away—a Type Two error.

"I didn't know whether it was loaded."
–Type One error

"I thought it was unloaded."
–Type Two error

Usually, Type Two errors are more serious.*

It was a cloudy night. Fred couldn't even see the Orion constellation or the asterism they call the Big Dipper.

He slowed to a walk. For the first time in his life, he figured out why he had never seen a blind person jogging.

Walking rather than running had one advantage and two disadvantages. The advantage was that he was less likely to fall and skin his knee.

The first disadvantage was that it would take him longer to get to the town.

---

* That's why the rule for firearms is: *Always treat every gun as if it were loaded.* That avoids the Category Two error of thinking it was unloaded when it was loaded.

The second was that, because he wasn't exercising as hard, he was going to feel cold more quickly.

Slower to town, quicker to freeze, Fred thought. He walked quickly.

In the next hour, all kinds of thoughts raced through his mind. *This is the 1855th day of my life. . . . I hope the people on the bus are okay. . . . I'm cold. . . . Betty is in Scotland. . . . I wish I were with her. . . . If lines l and m are concurrent, and lines m and n are concurrent, does that mean that l, m, and n are concurrent? . . . I'm really cold. . . . If a day starts out as Wednesday, will it stay Wednesday all day long? . . . Are prime numbers—2, 3, 5, 7, 11, 13, etc.—the same as prime rib? . . . Do ordinal numbers—first, second, third, etc.—like to take orders? . . . Who said A always gets to be first in the alphabet? . . . B, C, D, A, E, F. . . . I want to be a letter in the alphabet. . . . A, B, Fred, C, D, E. . . . One egg duck ticky-tock in furry socks.*

Two early signs of hypothermia* are sleepiness and mental confusion. Fred clearly qualified.

(Two later signs of hypothermia are loss of consciousness and death.)

---

* When body temperature drops more than 4°F (or about 2°C) below normal, which is 98.6°F (or 37°C).

Fred saw a pair of lights and thought it must be an airplane. He knew that when airplanes fly at night, they have a light on each wing.

Then he thought, *If I yell loud enough, the airplane will come down and land and save me.*

Then he realized that he was lying (not laying!) on the ground.

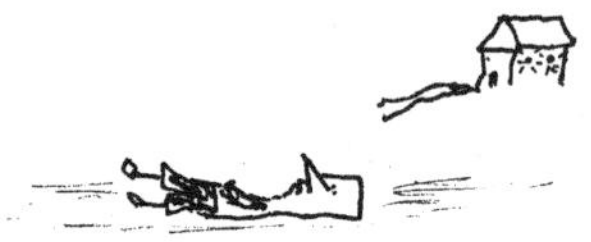

Fred stood up. The lights were on the ground and not in the sky. The lights were coming from a house.

Fred walked down the road to their mailbox and then down the path to the front door. He counted his steps as he walked: 1, 2, 3, 4, 5. He couldn't remember what came after 5. Fortunately, he kept walking.

By the time he got to the front door, his thoughts were totally muddled. He thought that standing in front of a door was enough to cause the door to be knocked. He waited and didn't hear any sound of knocking. He had forgotten that knocking on a door was a **voluntary action**. You have to actually do it.

In contrast, as he stood in front of the door, he thought *I have to remember to beat my heart.* He felt his pulse on his wrist and yelled, "Beat! Beat! Beat!" He "knew" he was causing his heart to beat. (A Category Two error.) Heart beating is an **involuntary action**.

Your Turn to Play

1. Is growing your fingernails or your hair a voluntary or involuntary action?
2. Is breathing a voluntary or involuntary action?
3. It's been about four chapters since we have introduced some new addition facts.

$$\begin{array}{r} \text{Chapter } 15 \\ -\quad 4 \\ \hline \text{Chapter } 11 \end{array}$$

Here are the numbers that add to 12:

$$\begin{array}{r} 3 \\ +\,9 \\ \hline 12 \end{array} \quad \begin{array}{r} 4 \\ +\,8 \\ \hline 12 \end{array} \quad \begin{array}{r} 5 \\ +\,7 \\ \hline 12 \end{array} \quad \begin{array}{r} 6 \\ +\,6 \\ \hline 12 \end{array} \quad \begin{array}{r} 7 \\ +\,5 \\ \hline 12 \end{array} \quad \begin{array}{r} 8 \\ +\,4 \\ \hline 12 \end{array} \quad \begin{array}{r} 9 \\ +\,3 \\ \hline 12 \end{array}$$

You already learned the doubles back in *Life of Fred: Dogs*. So we can eliminate 6 + 6 = 12. It's not new.

By the commutative law of addition we know that
3 + 9 will give the same answer as 9 + 3.
And 4 + 8 = 8 + 4, and 5 + 7 = 7 + 5.

So all you have to learn is 3 + 9 = 12, 4 + 8 = 12, and 5 + 7 = 12. Spend a minute and really learn those three facts. Please.

.......ANSWERS.......

1. You don't have to think about growing your fingernails or your hair. That happens automatically. Those are involuntary actions.

2. Breathing is strange. It will automatically happen. When you go to sleep at night, you keep on breathing, your heart keeps on beating, your fingernails keep on growing. Breathing is an involuntary action.

And yet, you can make it voluntary. You can take a big breath or you can hold your breath. You can make it a voluntary action.

3. Thank you.

Two of Fred's Silly Thoughts

#1: *Is ten miles longer in Missouri than in Kansas?*

Answer: No. But ten miles is longer in Kansas than in Texas. Explanation: The earth spins. Stand at the North Pole and you get turned around once every 24 hours. Stand at the equator and you're going about 1,000 miles per hour. You don't notice it, because the air is traveling along with you. Texas is south of Kansas. It's closer to the equator. Things in Texas are moving slightly faster than in Kansas. In high school physics you will learn about the Lorentz contraction: Things moving faster get very, very slightly shorter.

#2: *If a day starts out as Wednesday, will it stay Wednesday all day long?*

Answer: No. Not always. Midnight is not the only way to get from Wednesday to Thursday. All your life you have started a new day at one second after midnight.

But there is another way. Out in the Pacific Ocean is the International Date Line. Suppose you are on the right (east) side of that line and it's 2 p.m. on Wednesday. You cross that line. It will suddenly become 2 p.m. on Thursday. Swim back the other way, and it will become 2 p.m. Wednesday again.

Chapter Sixteen
Warm

The family was just sitting down for dinner. As was the custom in their prayer before the evening meal, each person named something that he or she was thankful for.

Tonight, the dad was grateful that the well pump was fixed today.

The mom was grateful for her three healthy sons.

The teenage son was thankful that mom had made a berry pie for dessert.

The dog barked.

"It's not your turn!" the nine-year-old told the dog. He was joking and everyone laughed. Prayer time at this house did not have to be super serious.

The dog barked again. He had heard Fred at the front door chanting, "Beat. Beat. Beat."

The dad went to the door and opened it. Fred looked up at the man and announced, "Randolf, the red shiny hose roof deer."

The man picked up Fred and brought him into the house. He put him in a chair by the fireplace and said to his family, "This little guy is an ice ball."

The mom threw a couple of blankets into the clothes dryer to heat them up. Then she wrapped Fred in the warm blankets.

The nine-year-old said, "Wouldn't it be quicker just to stick the kid in the microwave?" He liked to joke.

The seven-year-old brought Fred his cup of hot chocolate thinking that Fred might be hungry. Fred gratefully held it in his hands. It was warm. But, of course, he didn't drink it.

The mom looked at the black dot on his forehead. She peeled it off.

The dad explained to his sons, "The best thing to do is let him thaw out slowly. When someone's got hypothermia, you don't rush it."

They all headed back to the table and had dinner. Every couple of minutes the mom would get up and check on Fred. The color was slowly coming back into his cheeks. After dinner, the boys cleared off the table and the mom popped Fred into a warm bath.*

Fred had always showered at the KITTENS gym. Playing in the tub with bath toys was new to him.

* Not a hot bath.

In the hour that Fred was in the tub, the mom was going to wash Fred's clothes, but decided they didn't need washing. This was the first time she had ever seen a little boy's T-shirt without food stains on it. She didn't notice the $225 that Fred had in his pockets.

When Fred got out of the tub and put on his clean clothes, he felt like a new ~~man~~ boy. His fingers were all wrinkly.

Fred walked in the living room where the dad and his three sons were playing on the floor. Fred joined the circle.

The dad explained to Fred, "In the morning, the boys do their home schooling math. Our oldest is studying *Life of Fred: Calculus*." The teenager smiled. He had a little berry pie on the edges of his mouth.

The nine-year-old, who liked to joke, said, "And I'm also studying calculus." He held up his *Life of Fred: Cats* book. He had written the word *Calculus* on a piece of paper and had taped it over *Cats*.

Dad continued, "And in the evening we spend ten minutes playing the Addition Game. Watch us and you'll see how it's done."

There was a deck of cards in the middle of the circle. The dad had removed the tens, jacks, queens, and kings. All that was left were the ace, 2, 3, 4, 5, 6, 7, 8, and 9 of each suit. They pretended that the ace was a 1.

The seven-year-old was first. He drew two cards—a 5 and a 7—and said, "12." His dad smiled.

The nine-year-old drew two cards from the deck—an 8 and a 9—and said, "17."

To make things fair, the teenager had to draw three cards and add them. He drew 6, 9, and 6.

$$\begin{array}{r} 6 \\ 9 \\ +\ 6 \\ \hline 21 \end{array}$$

First, he added 6 and 9 and got 15.

Then 15 + 6: $\begin{array}{r} 15 \\ +\ 6 \\ \hline 21 \end{array}$

Fred's hands twitched. He was eager to play.

The dad said, "I know you're too young to do the addition. Take a card and see if you can read the number on the card."

Even though he was wearing his "Math Prof. KITTENS" T-shirt, the dad and the sons didn't realize who Fred was.

Fred picked up a  and said, "6." The dad patted him on his little square head and said, "Very good. You know your numbers."

Fred then picked up all 36 cards and said, "180."

Everyone was silent.

Fred said, "They add to 180."

Your Turn to Play

1. Fred dealt out all the hearts and then dealt out all the diamonds:

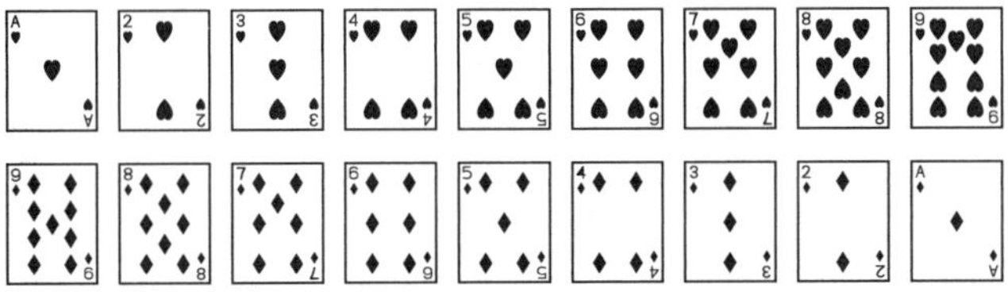

The diamonds were in reverse order.

Then he added them:

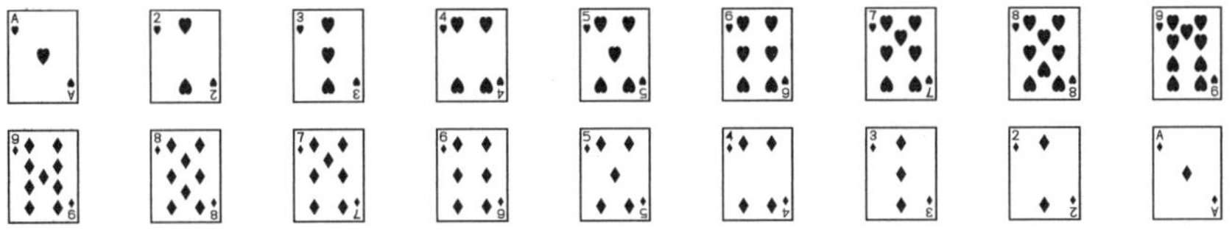

10 10 10 10 10 10 10 10 10

Your question: How many 10s did the red cards add up to?

2. How many 10s would the black cards (spades and clubs) add up to?

. . . . ANSWERS . . . .

1. There are nine 10s. That would add up to 90.
2. Similarly, there would be nine 10s for the black cards.

If the red cards added to 90, and the black cards added to 90, then

$$\begin{array}{r} 90 \\ +\ 90 \\ \hline 180 \end{array}$$

And that is how Fred knew all the cards added up to 180.

In case you are ever in Missouri in February and are invited to play the Addition Game . . .

A Row of Practice. *If your answers are not all correct, then get out a new sheet of paper and do the row again.*

$$\begin{array}{r} 9 \\ +\ 8 \\ \hline \end{array} \quad \begin{array}{r} 7 \\ +\ 5 \\ \hline \end{array} \quad \begin{array}{r} 4 \\ +\ 8 \\ \hline \end{array} \quad \begin{array}{r} 6 \\ +\ 9 \\ \hline \end{array} \quad \begin{array}{r} 3 \\ +\ 9 \\ \hline \end{array} \quad \begin{array}{r} 8 \\ +\ 8 \\ \hline \end{array} \quad \begin{array}{r} 6 \\ +\ 6 \\ \hline \end{array} \quad \begin{array}{r} 3 \\ +\ 7 \\ \hline \end{array}$$

17 12 12 15 12 16 12 10

Chapter Seventeen
A Family

This was all new to Fred. It was a family eating together, playing together, and enjoying each other. Fred had never experienced this before. It felt good.

After playing the Addition Game for ten minutes, they talked about what they would like to do next.

The seven-year-old brought out the Monopoly® game and said, "Let's play this, and he (pointing to Fred) will be on my side."

The dad smiled. This was perfect. When they had played it before, the seven-year-old had trouble making change with the Monopoly® money when he collected the rents. The dad knew that the kid with the square head would help him with the math.

The mom joined them. They opened the box and set up the board. There were five chairs and six people. Fred sat on the seven-year-old's lap.

The mom asked Fred if he had ever played Monopoly® before. "We can teach you," she offered.

"That's okay. Thank you. It probably won't be necessary," Fred answered. He was busy reading the rules that came with the game.

The teenager shook ⚄ ⚅ and moved 11 spaces on the board.

What a wonderful way to learn addition facts, Fred thought to himself.

They played. Fred and the seven-year-old had the Boardwalk monopoly. At Fred's suggestion, they traded it for the New York monopoly that the teenager had. The teenager thought that Fred was nuts. The Boardwalk property paid better rents.

Fred had noticed that people landed on New York much more frequently.

After Fred and the seven-year-old won the game, they all headed back to the living room to read for a while before bedtime.

The mom sat down next to Fred on the sofa. She had a stack of books in her arms for him. She also had a lot of questions that she wanted to ask.

She asked, "Are you hungry? I could warm you up some spaghetti that we had for dinner."

Fred answered, "I'm not hungry right now. Thank you."

"What's your name?"

"Fred Gauss."

"Fred, is there someone we can call to let them know that you are all right?* I'm sure that there must be someone who is concerned."

Fred thought for a moment. He knew that it would be silly to call Betty in Scotland. He knew that if they called his office, that Kingie would probably not answer the phone.

Fred explained that he didn't have a mother or father who was worried about where he was.

In his heart he wished that he was part of a family like the one he was with tonight. He would be happy to be their fourth son.

The father started wrestling with the two younger boys on the floor. The boys would jump on top of him. When one of the boys attacked the dad's left arm, the other attacked his legs. There was a lot of yelling and laughing.

Fred ached when he saw that.

---

* There is no such word as *alright.*
There are pairs of words like *all ready* and *already*
and *all together* and *altogether,*
but that doesn't happen with *all right.*

All ready and *already* have different meanings.
I am all ready (completely prepared) to enjoy some pizza.
I have eaten already (previously).

He wanted to be a part of that physical playing. He had had a childhood without much touching. He was put in front of the flickering blue parent (the television set).*

The Electric Babysitter

As a baby he just sat there with Kingie and watched either football, a romance channel, or a stock market report.

Nowadays, the flickering blue parent that offers no hugs is a computer or a little handheld gadget.

Fred looked at the stack of books that the mom had brought for them to read.

The first book shocked Fred a little. He had seen that somewhere before. He couldn't remember where.

He asked the mom if she had a copy of *Introduction to*

* The whole story is told in Chapter 6 of *Life of Fred: Calculus Expanded Edition.*

Metamathematics by Kleene. He had left his copy in his backpack on the bus.

She smiled and said, "I don't have that one, but I do have *Mary, the Moose from Missouri.*"

Fred shook his head.

Your Turn to Play

1. Instead, Fred suggested that they play Guess the Function. He started the game with these examples:

6 → 3 20 → 17 88 → 85 4 → 1 100 → 97

She asked him, "What am I supposed to do?"

He explained that she was supposed to find the rule that turned the first number into the second.

What was the rule?

2. It was her turn. These were her examples:

spoon → kitchen socks → bedroom saws → garage

tub → bathroom bowls → kitchen bed → bedroom

What was her rule?

3. Fred's turn:

spoon → 5 socks → 5 saws → 4 tub → 3

bowls → 5 bed → 3 Missouri → 8 it → 2

California → 10 somebody → 8 a → 1 sea → 3

What was his rule for the function?

4. The mom was starting to understand functions. She gave Fred one that she thought Fred wouldn't get.

mice → e rats → s meat → t somebody → y it → t

moose → e constellation → n Fred → d egg → g

What rule was she using?

.......ANSWERS.......

1. A function is a rule which associates to each thing exactly one answer.

For 6 → 3 20 → 17 88 → 85 4 → 1 100 → 97 the rule is subtract three.

When you get to algebra, we may write that rule as x → x – 3.

2. The rule for spoon → kitchen socks → bedroom, etc. is associate to each thing the room of the house where the item is most commonly kept.

3. The rule for spoon → 5 socks → 5 saws → 4, etc. is associate with each word the number of letters in it.

4. The rule for mice → e rats → s meat → t, etc. is associate to each word the last letter of the word.

a small essay

Functions

The idea of functions is at the heart of much of math. In arithmetic, you have been learning about a special function that takes ordered pairs of numbers and gives you an answer.

For example, (3, 6) → 9 (7, 8) → 15 (9, 2) → 11 (100, 2) → 102 (2, 2) → 4 (5, 8) → 13 (4, 20) → 24.

The name of this function is called addition.

A second function in arithmetic is subtraction. Later in arithmetic will be multiplication and division.

In trigonometry we will have the tangent function. In calculus we will have the derivative function.

Chapter Eighteen
To Edgewood

Fred explained to the mom that he had been on a bus headed to Edgewood. The bus had broken down, and he had run on ahead to the repair station to find someone to fix it.

When the dad had stopped wrestling with the boys, she asked him, "Max, have you heard anything about a bus that broke down?"

"Yes," he said. "We got a call late this afternoon. A bus with a broken fuel line. I'm scheduled to fix it tomorrow morning."

❁ ❁ ❁

The mom had made a bed for Fred on the sofa and gave him lots of blankets and a pillow. She kissed him on the forehead. He was soon asleep.

❁ ❁ ❁

The next morning was Thursday. Fred awoke to the sounds of family life. The mom was busy making breakfast. The dad was in the bathroom using an electric shaver. The nine-year-old was asking his younger brother, "Did you hear the joke about the moose that had three feet? It was out in the yard! Ha! Ha! Ha!" The seven-year-old didn't think it was funny.

Breakfast was bacon, eggs, pancakes, and large glasses of milk. Fred put a piece of bacon in his pocket "for later." He shared the rest with the teenage boy who gladly devoured it.

❀ ❀ ❀

By 7:20 Max and Fred were at the bus.

One window of the bus was decorated with black dots. Fred knew who had put them there.

Max repaired the fuel line and put enough diesel in the bus so that they could get to the next town and fill up.

Max left to get to work at the repair station. Fred looked out the back window of the bus and waved to him. Fred thought, *I want to be a dad like him when I grow up.*

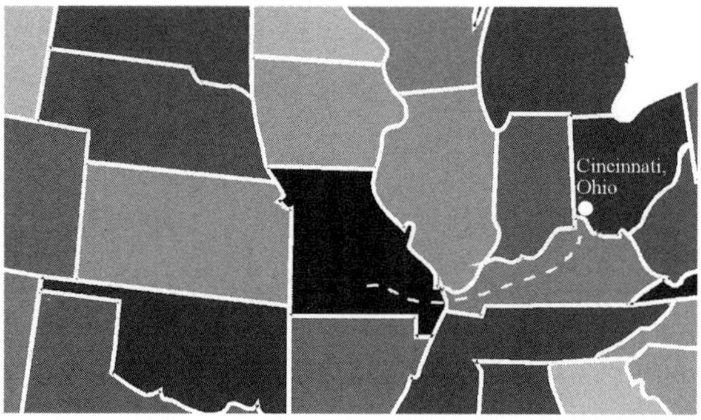

The bus was in Missouri heading east (⇢). It would soon be in Kentucky.

Then it would swing north (↑) toward the big city of Cincinnati, which is in Ohio.

Edgewood, Kentucky, is about 10 miles south of Cincinnati.

Fred read his metamathematics book until the bus arrived at Edgewood. The two-year-old just played with her dots and didn't bother Fred.

It was in the afternoon when the bus rolled into Edgewood. Fred put away his book, put on his backpack, and stepped off the bus. Everyone else stayed on the bus. They were heading to Cincinnati.

The bus left. Fred stood there. He didn't know what to do. The KITTENS president had said that the students and faculty "have not seen enough of the world." The campus computer had assigned Fred to see Edgewood. There he was. Edgewood, Kentucky. The population is about nine thousand (cardinal number). The area is a little over four square miles.

In the city, the median age is 38 years. That means that half of the population is younger than 38, and half is older than 38.

The median average income for a family in Edgewood is \$80,578 according to the 2000 census. That means that half of the families make less than \$80,578, and half make more.

Only one percent of those older than 65 were poor ("below the poverty line").

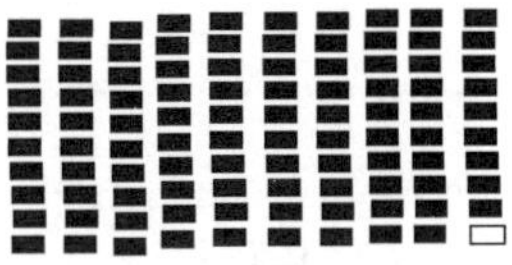

One percent = 1% = one out of a hundred ↗

Fred started walking. He didn't know what else to do. He walked past Caywood Elementary School. All of the kids playing in the schoolyard were bigger than he was.

A block away was Turkeyfoot Middle School. He couldn't imagine why the school was named "Turkeyfoot." Then he realized that the school was on Turkeyfoot Road.*

Thirty-seven percent of the people in Edgewood were under 25 years old. The rest (63%) were 25 and older.

$$\begin{array}{r} 37\% \\ +\ 63\% \\ \hline 100\% \end{array}$$

In a bar graph:

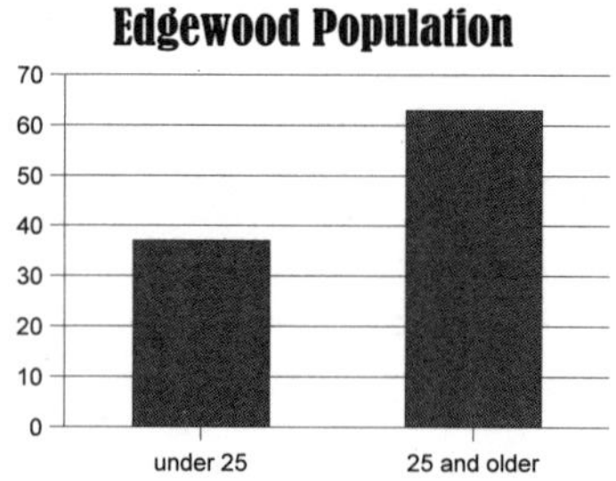

Fred was feeling very alone. He thought about being back with Max and his family. Or back at KITTENS.

He walked down Dudley Road and turned left on Dixie Highway. He found a Circle K grocery store and bought the local newspaper.

He read about the Youth Dance Party, but that was for kids in grades 4–6. He read about the Edgewood Night at the roller skating rink,

* These schools are real. Edgewood is real. Turkeyfoot Middle School is located at 3230 Turkeyfoot Road, Edgewood KY 41017-2645.

but the event was "for Edgewood residents only." The Snow Tubing at Perfect North Slopes was next week.

Fred made the mistake of not talking with anyone. He was just wandering the streets, not knowing what to do. He was lonely. Many of the people in Edgewood would have welcomed him as warmly as Max and his family in Missouri had done.

Your Turn to Play

1. If you live in a town of 61 people of differing heights and you are as tall as the median height, how many people in that city are shorter than you are?

2. If 20% of the people in that city own a pet, what percent do not own a pet?

3. Edgewood is about ten miles south of Cincinnati. What direction would you head to go from Edgewood to Cincinnati?

4. 83640
 + 47257

5. Give an example of a set whose cardinality is 3.

.......ANSWERS.......

1. If you are as tall as the median height, then half the people are shorter than you. In a town of 61 people, 30 of them would be shorter than you. (And 30 would be taller than you.)

2. If 20% own a pet, then 80% do not own a pet.

$$\begin{array}{r} 20\% \\ +\ 80\% \\ \hline 100\% \end{array}$$

3.

4.

$$\begin{array}{r} \overset{1}{8}3640 \\ +\ 47257 \\ \hline 130897 \end{array}$$

You start on the right. 0 + 7 = 7
Then 4 + 5 = 9, and 6 + 2 = 8.
When you add 3 + 7 you get 10. You write down the 0 and carry the one.
1 + 8 = 9 and 9 + 4 = 13.

5. I thought of these examples: {5, 982, 44069311283}, {♪, ⌚, ✈}, {L, M, N}, and {🍦, 🥕, 🗑}.

I bet your answer was different than any of my examples.

Chapter Nineteen
To KITTENS

Fred saw airplanes flying overhead. (Which word in the previous sentence is superfluous*?)

As he looked at the airplanes, he thought about how nice it would be to head home right now. One of the planes was coming in for a landing. Fred was very close to an airport.

From the grocery store he walked to the airport. A big sign announced:

Cincinnati–Northern Kentucky International Airport.

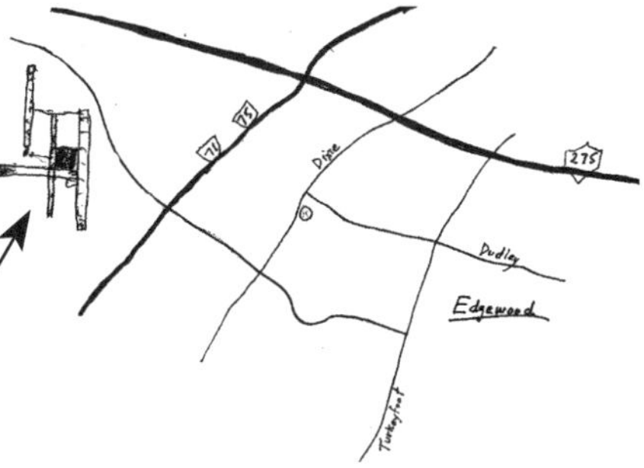

Inside the airport terminal people were rushing around. They all looked like they knew what they were doing. This was all new to Fred.

So many airlines! Everything from AAAAA Airways to Zippo Flights. Which line do I stand in?

He spotted the sign: Information ☞

---

*(sue-PER-flew-us) Superfluous = extra, redundant.
"Super" means above or beyond.
"Fluous" comes from the Latin *fluere*, which means to flow.

Fred rushed over to the booth. He didn't know what to say. He was so grateful to have someone to talk to.

He just said, "Help!"

"How may I help you?" she answered.

"I want to go to KITTENS," Fred said.

"I don't understand. Do you want to go to the petting zoo or to a pet store?" she said. Her voice sounded like it was recorded.

"No. The real KITTENS. I want to go to KITTENS University," he explained.

"I cannot help you matriculate.* Please tell me where you would like to travel to," she said.

"I want to travel to KITTENS University."

"I'm sorry. That city is not in my data base."

Fred suddenly realized that he was talking to a robot. Her arms never moved. Her eyes never blinked.

"Does any airline at this airport go to Kansas?"

"Yes. We have <pause> one airline. It is <pause> Dottie Charter."

---

* mah-TRICK-you-late To matriculate is to enroll as a student at a college.

Fred thanked the robot. (It was a habit of his—being polite.)

He ran past AAAAA Airways. Past Butterfly Flights. He arrived at . . .

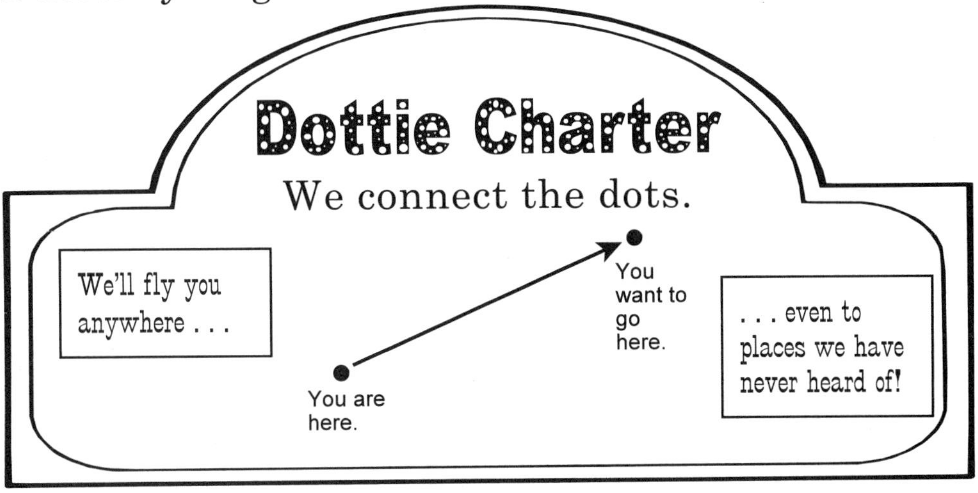
Dottie Charter
We connect the dots.
We'll fly you anywhere . . .
You are here.
You want to go here.
. . . even to places we have never heard of!

He raced up to the ticket counter and asked, "Can you get me to KITTENS University?"

The agent smiled. "Of course," she said. "This is a charter airline. We can take you to any spot you like."

She blinked. She smiled. She wasn't a robot.

"That will be $40 for the flight."

Fred took eight five-dollar bills out of one of his pockets. 5, 10, 15, 20, 25, 30, 35, 40.

The agent handed him a ticket and told him to head out gate 314 and pick any **Dottie** plane he liked.

Fred was expecting ⇢ 

Instead, **Dottie**, herself, would take Fred wherever he wished. Fred climbed on her back and pointed west.

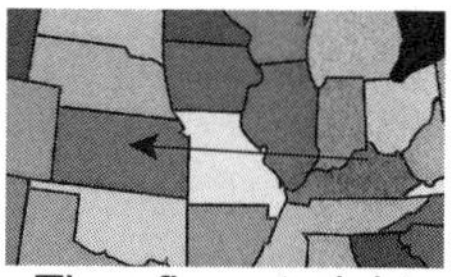

They flew straight as the duck flies

Dottie landed right in front of the Math Building and Fred hopped off.

He ran up the two flights of stairs and down the hallway past the nine vending machines (four on one side and five on the other).

When Fred entered his office, Kingie was just finishing up his last oil painting of the day.

Kingie asked nervously, "Did you bring any cats or dogs with you?" Kingie was ready to dash to his fort for protection.

"No. Just me. I'm glad to be home," Fred answered.

He set down his backpack, gave Kingie a hug, and headed to bed.

In his backpack . . .

Index

Index

After you read the *Life of Fred: Elementary Series* books, there are *Life of Fred* books that will take you all the way up into your fourth year of college.

Celebrate that good news!

If you would like to learn more about books written about Fred . . .

FredGauss.com